I AM THE KEY THAT OPENS ALL DOORS

I dedicate this work to all the souls that have helped me grow immensely along the way, inspired me throughout every step of my life and to every reader that was drawn from within to take the journey that will take him/her and all of us to the same destination. And may you continue your journey quest to live happily ever after.

CONTENTS

DISCLAMER

This work is solely for personal growth, education and recreation. It is not a therapeutic activity such as counseling or medical advice and should not be treated as a substitute for any professional advice. In the event of any physical distress, please consult with appropriate professionals. The information and the application of any protocols in this book is the choice of each reader, who assumes full responsibility for his or her understandings, interpretations and results.

The author assumes no responsibility for the actions or choices of any reader. While all attempts have been made to verify the information provided in this publication, neither the author nor the publisher assumes any responsibility for errors, omissions or contrary interpretations of the subject matter herein. No part of this publication may be reproduced, stored in a retrieval system, or transmitted in any form or by any means, electronic, mechanical, photocopying, recording or otherwise, without the written permission of the author.

Reviewers may quote brief passages in reviews. The author of this book does not dispense medical advice or prescribe the use of any technique as a form of treatment for physical, emotional or medical problems without the advice of a physician, either directly or indirectly. The intent of the author is only to offer information of a general nature to help you in your quest for mental, emotional and spiritual well-being and clarity. In the event you use any information in this book for yourself, the author assumes no responsibility for your actions. All artworks in the paperback version created by Saimir Kercanaj. Book cover created by the author through "Canva".

ISBN :9798508537845

Other books by the author:

BODY MIND SOUL: AS YOU BELIEVE, SO SHALL IT BE
https://www.amazon.com/dp/B09NNQLK25

SELF EMPOWERMENT: BOOK 1
https://www.amazon.com/dp/B09RWBCWCP

LIMITLESS POTENTIAL. *Journey to self realization*
https://www.amazon.com/dp/B09Z37B2QR

BECOME FREE THROUGH INSIGHTFUL POETRY
https://www.amazon.com/dp/B0B1CXR8C1

YOU ARE NOT A STRAWMAN YOU ARE THE ZYGOTE
https://www.amazon.com/dp/B0BT6YF2XS

GAIN WISDOM THROUGH PRACTICED KNOWLEDGE

FOREWORD

The creation process of any art form is an interesting phenomenon. It is a process with lots of bumps along the way. Writing this book has been an immense effort on my part. Although I draw and paint, writing a book is a totally new art form that requires nerves of steel. It requires will and determination. It requires many sleepless nights and it also requires having a pen and paper with you at all times. There is nothing new under the sun. Everything was already said and done a long time ago. It's a matter of perception and interpretation. It is an easy-to-read book. And not scientifically written. I wanted to write the book as if we were talking face to face. Something being professional is a capitalism term in which certain people decide what professional is. If you were to write this book by using your way of thinking, then it would be a different book, so that is why I wanted to write it based on how I perceive things as a writer and as a reader. I mention this because many people that struggle in life mentally or emotionally have fallen prey to their own expectations.

Many beautiful things in life get unnoticed or not enjoyed because of the expectations that we have about them. When you have no expectations, you only get rewarded. This is an absolute fact. I stopped writing a few times along the way and yet something inside of me pushed me to keep going. My intention to do my part in the betterment of our civilization was extraordinarily strong for me to give up. I never give up and it is not an ego thing when it is about having a strong determination to improve my life and others'. We humans have great potential when we are truly aligned with our real selves. Nothing can stop us.

No such thing as nonsense or science fiction. Science fiction is considered when we lack inner standing. If you can imagine something, you can materialize it. Your imagination is the limit. Imagination is more important than knowledge. Knowing something, you will only live your life based only on what you already know.

And you will most likely be living a boring life because you will just be replaying your everyday habits. When imagination is in play, when you are curious to know, you put more variety of flavor (paints) into your life (painting). Why is a child happier compared to an adult? One word "IMAGINATION". They are always curious to know, that's why they always have questions.

As adults, we are so tired of our boring uninspiring life that we tell (or think in our heads) children to shut up or stop asking this or that when they question constantly. Do you want to be happy? Be a child. Have questions, imagine, search the unknown and you will see.

You always learn. There must be a constant curiosity for knowledge and inner standing. I learned a lot in writing this book. Remember that no matter how much you know and innerstand, if you are barren of compassion, then the knowledge (which can tempt you to become greedy, angry, envy etc.) will destroy you sooner or later. At the end of the book where all the artworks are, you will see that a few of them have triangles. You might think it is an illuminati sign, but it isn't. The triangle is the mother, father, son relation- TRINITY.

Also, the triangle pointing up is the male (phallus) symbol, and the one pointing down is the female symbol in esoteric knowledge. DO NOT skip any chapter or page if you don't innerstand something or get triggered. They are all related to each other in the grand scheme of things, regardless if you believe or innerstand certain things written or not. Besides, anything that may trigger your emotions, is a part of you that needs to be healed. Do not let your body become the mind. The book must be read in its entirety. Even if you don't innerstand or believe certain things. Even if some chapters may seem like they don't relate to each other, they do. Life is a philosophy. You may innerstand something right away or later after repetition of mistakes until you finally learn. If some things in this book may seem like they are far out of reach, they are not. As I have mentioned in one of the chapters, you must be a sniper and see things from an eagle's perspective. See the bigger picture. I purposefully included a chapter that seems like it is totally off, and yet, it isn't at all when you become an eagle.

My intention is to make you think. Throughout the book I use the word "innerstand" instead of "understand". To Understand means to stand under (someone else's) authority. While the word inner standing means understanding from within, under no external authority. You are your own authority. Do not get attached to things. There is a little story when Albert Einstein was leaving Nazi Germany for America. His wife was overly concerned that she had to leave behind much of her things. "I'm attached to them," she said. To this, Albert said,

"But my dear, they are not attached to you" Do not get attached to anything. Attachment will be your demise. Throughout this book there is a lot of philosophical and spiritual advice that you can put in practice and have immediate results if you really are a determined person. There is no "IF". You are a determined person. You just need to realize it consciously. See life as a play and not as a job. And only then will you overcome many non-existent problems created in your mind by being attached to a non-existent past and/ or future.

In this or my other books I use words such as: Maybe, perhaps, possibly, allegedly, it is a fact, an absolute truth and other similar words or phrases. It is a personal opinion or fact. You, as a reader treat this or any other book like you would any fictional book so that you do not fall in the trap of satisfying personal beliefs and expectations where you'll end up rejecting information that would eventually prove to be detrimental to you, as opposed to keeping an open mind, which would reward you. When you have no expectations, then I guarantee that you will learn a thing or two from every single book in existence.

**<u>English is not the author's mother language.
The message is clear in this book.</u>**

I AM

THE KEY THAT OPENS ALL DOORS

journey to peace and freedom

SAIMIR KERCANAJ

" *Oh star, Oh **SUN**, may the rays of **Rah** shine brilliant and strong. May the hours of Horus step daily and long. Be strength for us all like the sky to the dove and may you always be the star of **Light**, **Life** and **Love**"*

- ::Joseph-James:Szyszka

1

WHO AM I?

"I know that I AM intelligent, because I know that I know nothing. -*Socrates*

Who are you? A question for you to ask yourself. Give it a try and ask yourself who you are. What would the answer be? Most likely you will answer by defining yourself as an identity. Giving yourself a title, such as being John, Mary or Bob. The average person will answer with their name or last name. Your name and last name are given to you by your parents, but you are not that name and last name. Well, you might look at yourself and say that is you, but that's not you either. That is your body. Then, "Who are you?". It is a remarkably interesting question.

You live simultaneously in three different planes of inner standing; You are a spiritual creature; have an intellect and you live in a physical body. But because you lack awareness and inner standing of who you are, you are totally locked in the physical world. You let things (other people's opinions or situations that are beyond your control) outside of you control you. The majority of the population are reacting to life and are not really living at all. Your life revolves around defining you as your job, your car, your house, your nationality etc.

You think you are those things, but those things you think you are, is an illusion and bizarre. It's your lower self " EGO" and your external make-up, which makes you think you are those things, but you are not, and it holds you and those around you back. Unfortunately, from the cradle, the whole human species has been programmed into a low vibrational 3D consciousness, with strong contrasts, duality, limitations, emotional triggers and ego-centric behaviors.

Our moods can swing quickly from happiness, bliss, fun and joy into despair, rejection, sadness, pain, apathy, guilt, shame, indecision, blocks, procrastination and fear.

This is very destructive to your life, your well-being and personal power. We all have experienced these emotions and know how debilitating they can be when we don't work on mitigating them. Those low frequency traits can make you emotional. All human emotions are preceded by thoughts. You can't have an emotion without having thoughts about it first. Consciously or subconsciously. Emotions are learned behaviors. Behaviors are learned since childhood, and even further back in the womb.

By the end of this book, you should realize if you have the potential to grow physically (health wise), mentally, emotionally and spiritually. I believe you do, otherwise you would have not been interested in this kind of book. Many people never analyze themselves. Mentally they are mechanical products of their environment, preoccupied with breakfast, and going here and there to be entertained.

They don't know what they are seeking, nor why,. They never realize complete happiness and lasting satisfaction. By evading self-analysis, people go on being robots, conditioned by their environment. True self-analysis is the greatest art of progress. Are you one of those people.? You are not your Ego's hostage. So, WHO ARE you? To know who you are, you need to first unlearn all the distorted useless ways of life that are part of this matrix created by the beings residing in the lower astral realm of the fourth dimension.

To innerstand who you are you must not only question your physical reality, but also the metaphysical part of it.

This book has quite a lot of metaphysical content to make you question the opposite side of the physical reality, the unseen which is always present. When you innerstand how amazingly and intelligently you are designed, you may ask yourself: "Why are we suffering as a species? Why wars, hate, famine, fear etc.? Could it be that hidden hands are behind all the suffering pulling the strings? Is our pure ignorance getting taken advantage of? Are you an ignorant or an intelligent person? I think you, and only you can truly answer this question.

Have an open mind that everything is possible, but believe no one, follow your intuition. Anything I, or others say, will only satisfy or dissatisfy you with opinions. Is your life a dream? The truth is, only the person that dreams knows the meaning of it. Your higher self will always reply with the truth. Your higher self is not judgmental.

You are the son/daughter of the light and brother of the darkness, aren't you? It is you that must figure out who you really are. Total health must be your aim. Physical, mental and spiritual health. I elaborate further on all these in my other book: "**MIND BODY SOUL: As you believe, so shall it be**"

Be humble enough to know that you are not better than anyone else, yet wise enough to innerstand and know that you are different than the rest. Within yourself, on a soul level you are the same as everyone else (on an energetic/frequency level) or different than everyone externally. So, who are you then? Try answering without a name, job, status, achievement etc. The answer may lie with how well you can communicate with yourself. If you cannot communicate with yourself, how would you know who you are. The deeper you go within, the more you will want to be by yourself.

> *Nobody can innerstand the depth of your thoughts and feelings. It is time that you start looking inward and ask yourself the big question: "WHO AM I?" You must question both intellectually and spiritually. Don't force it. Getting rid of a desire is a desire. You and only you know the path and rhythm of finding the answer. I believe that you must go through something that absolutely destroys you so you can figure out who you really are.*

After you have destroyed yourself and asked this question again, maybe you will answer with:

"I AM eternal life and mystery"
"I am who I am meant to be"
"I am free"
"I am"

A young man asked a monk, "What is Ego?"

The monk in turn asked him, "Who are you"

"Well" replied the young man, giving his name, 'Mohan.'

"I'm not asking your name; I want to know who you are" countered the monk.

"I am a student", said the young man.

"But that is your present station or profession in life-my question is-who are you?"

The young man thought for a while and then said: "I am the son of so-and-oo."

"That is your relationship with your parents" smiled the monk.

"I am Bengali", said the young man.

"That is your mother-tongue"

"I am a Hindu and an Indian"

"That is your religion and nationality"

"I am a human being", the young man reached his wit's end.

"Now, you are referring to the species"-The Homo Sapiens. Who are you?"

The young man had nothing more to say.

"Well, that is what Vedanta teaches," continued the monk. The Vedanta says that man's deepest core or substance within, is unconditional by any description and that unconditioned substance is called Atman or SELF. The Atman is what a man is. Ego is what appears to be. Atman is true, Ego is false. Atman (or SELF) is never born nor dies; Ego comes into being through ignorance and dies when knowledge dawns in a person

---

When ego dies, a new 'you' is reborn. Death can come in many forms. Besides 'ego death', another example of death is in the form of wasting the sexual energy/life force. In the book *You Are The One* by Pine G. Land the author had this to say:

When the expulsion of semen happens, an induction happens, in a form of male reproductive cycle.

The author continues on saying that:

This reproductive cycle can also be seen as a male period. You may see the word "period" as nonsense because you associate that

word only with women but try to understand the bigger picture. In men, every time an orgasm (including the ejaculation) happens, there are psychological consequences. Just as women have psychological/ emotional consequences during their menstrual cycle or period. These emotional consequences manifest as depression, irritability, fatigue, mood fluctuations, less concentration, heightened impatience and also removing themselves from society, it makes them vulnerable

Affirm to yourself daily "*I AM intelligent because I know that I know nothing.*" Don't let those who cannot see, convince you that you are hallucinating. Daily affirmations are crucial to align yourself with your soul/ higher self. The chapter about subconsciousness will explain the importance of it.

AFFIRMATIONS

- I AM not what people want me to be.

- I AM what I AM meant to be.

- I AM eternal life and mystery.

- I AM you and YOU are me.

- I AM brave, fearless and FREE.

- I AM everything I want to see.

- I AM the sacred Love that rests in me.

2

ARE YOU A HUMAN OR AN EXTRA-TERRESTRIAL?

Whether you are a human or an extra-terrestrial, depends on how you picture your reality. If you think you are a human, then it means that you have lost your spirituality and you must strive for obtaining it. To obtain it, you must stop being a human. What does "*must stop being a human*" mean? Well, it is not that you will die, or disappear in thin air or something. It is all about your consciousness. It is about expanding beyond what you have lived your life so far. You must not be driven by Earthly redundancy. Do not be driven by materialism, sex, power etc.

You must have a higher purpose for existing.

If you are an E.T., then you are a spiritual force in the Universe that is channelling itself through your human embodiment to serve the planet and its course of evolution in the consciousness ladder. You decide whether you are a human body, or whether you are a spirit dressed in a meaty flesh/ physical body. The Universe rearranges itself to serve your picture of reality.

Anything you strive to be, the Universe will make sure to serve you by fulfilling your wishes and desires. It is how it works. If things you desire do not get accomplished, it is because you have not innerstood what you are. The Universe/Creator is your servant in the sense that because you are created from Love, you will have been given *FREE WILL* which is 'Love'. Someone that loves you, will let you choose freely without constraints, right? Why do you think that the extra-terrestrials in movies or fake news are mostly portrayed as ugly/mean creatures?

That's because those that control the content of the movies, do not want you to realize who you really are. "As you believe so shall it be" is a powerful Universal law which dictates "what you beLIEve, becomes your reality". Don't you think it is time to question your beliefs about the Extra-terrestrials?

What are you, a human being or an Extra-terrestrial? Your answer will determine your destination. Your answer will determine whether you will move up higher in the consciousness/reality ladder or whether you will stay where you are (for now).

The only major problem that can slow you down to expand your consciousness, is whether you believe in reincarnation. If you don't believe in reincarnation, then clearly you are a human being, but if you do believe in reincarnation, then you are a spiritual person and will progress much, much faster than those that believe that life is only birth and death (one life and that's it). Know that on the 5th dimension you are a Christ Consciousness being.

- **PLANE**t (plane/flat realm?)

- plan**ET** (ET's plan?)

- Extra Terra = Extra Land

- Extra Terrestrial/ET = Beings from beyond the official known Earth land/ map.

Are we dreaming to be having a physical experience in this Earth? When we physically die, do we actually awake from this dream? A dream looks so real, what makes you think that this life is not a dream?

You came here (not necessarily physically but your spirit came from somewhere else to be having a physical experience in this realm) to bring your love, light and wisdom to assist the planet in its transition from 3d to 5D. Many have just forgotten the mission in helping guiding humanity toward a bright future. You will remember, I guarantee. I strongly suggest that you write down your dreams and any particular situation that happens in your everyday life. They are messages. Even if they may not seem important, write them down anyway. They will be useful at the right time and at the right place.

There have always been Extra-terrestrials on Earth. A big influx has happened in recent decades. They have lent their consciousness to Earthly humans to assist in the transition. Have you noticed that more and more people are awakening from a coma? That is because of two reasons as far as I can tell:

1- Benevolent otherworldly beings lending their consciousness to Earthly humans.

2-   As per the 100th monkey effect, when a specific number of people learns something new, the new acquired knowledge will be automatically learned by other people.

You may ask yourself: How come those people that didn't learn, will know the things that the others did? That is because the information is energy. Time and space does not exist for the energy. So, the information will be transferred telepathically between people. Now, you might have a question that: If this is true, then how come there are still a lot of people that are asleep and have no clue about the true reality of our system?

That is because those people refuse to wake up, which means that most likely they will be reincarnated again on a 3d like realm just like Earth. Well, Earth is not in 3D frequency anymore. 3D reality ended in 2012. We are now In the transitioning period. Most of us were asleep years ago. How come we woke up in these times? We remembered who we are. Something triggered an awakening in us. I'm assuming you are awake (to a certain point).

If you are not awake, having this book in your hand, can assure you that you are on the right track. Nothing is a coincidence my Extra-terrestrial friend. Earth is a school. Not your home. If you think that this realm (not planet) is your home, then that makes you a human. I will ask one more time:

Are you a human or an Extra-terrestrial?

3

PLANDEMIC/SCAMDEMIC

The greatest hoax in known human history. The powers that be managed and convinced most of the world to kneel without firing a single bullet.

According to the mind control establishment a.k.a government (Footnote#1), fast food stores, big box stores are essential to public health but gyms, recreation centers and small businesses had to close down because they were not essential for our health. Apparently, the virus does not spread at junk food stores or any other big corporate store. If it was not a multinational corporation business, it had to close down or else the virus (the pretend virus) would be spreading throughout small businesses, according to the powers that be which have 100% conflict of interest if a small business stays open. Hmm, I wonder why? (Rhetorical question. The cause of this, at least one of the reasons was to destroy small businesses. People consuming junk food causes them to get sick easier.

This way THEY could further their agenda to depopulate us. I strongly recommend you watch the 2006 movie "IDIOCRACY". It is categorized under comedy/sci-fi, but it's so truthful about our society's current situation. The plot of the movie seems exaggerated, but it's spot on. To me, it was a documentary. This supposed virus or flu strain with a survival rate of over 90% created a big impact mentally on the majority of the population. It was all mental.

This supposed virus was not as dangerous as they made it out to be. People die every day, that's how nature recycles itself. It is the life cycle. People get so carried away and distracted with meaningless stuff that they forget to live in the moment. They are distracted about death, which is perfectly normal everyday occurrence.

If the media would always report saily on how many people die from cancer, accidents or any other diseases, then it would be considered a pandemic. When this virus thing started, all of a sudden, the media everywhere in the world reported it and bombarded humanity constantly. It created a new beLIEf in most, the beLIEf that it was real. It was not. It was only real in people's head. I was an essential worker in the food industry, and nothing happened to me or anyone I know.

Out of everyone that I knew, only one of them had someone that died from the supposed virus. Even if they died from Covid, it does not mean it was dangerous on a global scale with all those padded numbers. For example, if someone died from a helicopter fall, it probably would have been ruled as a CONvid death. That person could have very easily had a weak immune system or other comorbidities.

Someone that might seem healthy to you, does not necessarily mean that they are. They could be struggling inside from many emotional or mental problems. Many wear a social mask metaphorically speaking and you cannot tell how they feel inside. It was ridiculous that people who wore a muzzle (mask), bought food that was touched by who knows how many people, starting from the factory to the delivery workers to the final destination workers and finally customers touching the product.

You pay at the cash register surrounded by plexiglass, while the cashier was touching all the stuff you just bought. As if the virus was so stupid that it couldn't curve around the plexiglass. The virus could enter through your nose, eyes, ears and skin. Yes, your skin is full of tiny holes. There was no virus (except the media). Just a flu, less deadly than a regular flu but you get sick faster. Every year millions die from the flu. Why don't people protest about it? Most people are glued to their devices and other meaningless distracting things. No protests, unless the media tricks you into protesting about the opposite of what really matters.

They have played you like a fiddle. Breathing with a mask on is harmful to your health. Even without a mask on, we as humans in general, are breathing with our chest, meaning short irregular breaths. This is caused by living everyday life in an anxious and stressful environment. Breathing with a mask on you puts stress on your overall body health. People were saying they felt fine breathing for hours. Now, I say, breathing with a mask on does not mean you will lose an arm or a leg but the damage is done incrementally over a period of time.

If you don't allow your body to absorb enough oxygen at a regular rate that the brain and body needs, it will harm your brain and endocrine system in the long run. If not enough oxygen goes to the brain, you will become less intelligent. By breathing in your own carbon dioxide, you are putting back into your lungs the pathogens, bacteria and opportunistic organisms that were supposed to exit. There is a cycle that must happen, in and out .

We inhale air, and exhale carbon dioxide. The Creator created us perfectly. If you are scared your whole life, you clearly have no idea how powerful a creature you are. You are capable of thinking for yourself. There was no virus. At least not the virus that the media worldwide shouted from the rooftops. The only deadly virus that existed was in your head. You may be walking, talking etc., but it does not mean you that you are healthy mentally and/or emotionally.

You might be dead inside, but you don't have to be.

Your external (physical body) is just as important as being healthy mentally and emotionally. People use science to express their opinion by describing how this virus works, like droplets from coughing can travel a certain distance in the air and many other nonsenses.

Those are all left brain $cience/$tatism explanations. Look around you and within yourself. Think and feel unconditionally and you will realize life is simple and beautiful. There is nothing to fear. Anything that you think, you can manifest. If you think about death constantly, you will manifest death, literally or metaphorically . You could think about happiness and stay away from people that live in fear and you will manifest happiness.

Do not let "the powers that be" or people that operate in fear, dictate how you feel or act. All this fear that they impose on people is to advance their depopulation agenda. Overpopulation is a myth. In fact, there is so much land on Earth that if everyone lived as densely as New York City, the entire world population could fit in an area the size of Texas or almost three times the population could fit in Alaska. The lie that we are overpopulated is spread to induce fear and scarcity over the masses. They (the powers that be) use many ways/tactics to lower the population. It is a statistical fact that 50% of humans live on less than 1% of the Earth's land . For those that are allergic to geography, only India and China have a combined population of 2.7 billion based on the official (could be made up) numbers. Earth's total land area is only what the official narrative says. I'll leave it up to your imagination and critical thinking abilities to think outside the box. Personally, I don't believe at all that the world population is 7-8 billion.

I believe we are way less. The lie is so they can progress their depopulation control agenda. If a fraction of the lawns were turned into gardens, food scarcity would be non-existent. Many that don't know the facts, say that we are overpopulated because we use resources way faster than they generate. This is not true at all. Here are some examples :

1-The amount of forests today on Earth is way bigger than let's say 200 year ago. 200 years ago, about 90% of the North American east coast from Quebec (Canada) to Florida (U.S.A.) was completely clear cut. Today it is full of trees. Same with most of Europe. Trees have grown back.

2-The world getting destroyed by oil, is not true at all. 40% of America's oil, the biggest oil consumer on Earth, comes from Canada, which is the most ethically sourced oil on Earth. Oil is ABIOTIC, meaning it will absolutely never run out. It cannot run out. Oil is being regenerated at all times from within Earth's mantle. The lie that oil runs out, was started in 1892, they conditioned people to believe that oil comes from fossils. The truth is that it's replenishing every day and will never run out.

3-There exists technologies today that have been suppressed from the public. Such technologies could put every single energy industry out of business overnight. There are nuclear reactors the size of small home appliance systems that could power the entirety of North America for 100 years without needing more fuel. This technology was discovered from the Roswell New Mexico crash, where a spacecraft was given/seeded to the American government by off-world entities, known as the Greys (created by the reptilians or Archons).

That was a deliberate seeding of technology and not an accident. The military refers to off-world technology as *"exotic technology"* and not "alien technology". This technology is hidden because there exists a group of entities (not humans) that operate in low vibration and frequency that wish to enslave humanity. Humanity cannot be enslaved if this technology were released to the masses.

4-Most agriculture is environmentally destructive due to modern day farming practices. However, if we adopted natural farming methods, such as No-Till Farming, which boosts yield and growth rate by 200% we could feed the world population many times over.

5- Primary water cycle. Water is a renewable source just like oil. It can never run out. All the scarcity promoted throughout decades, is nothing more than to control human life. They can control the prices and taxes however they deem fit. We as a human species have been conditioned to beLIEve that the above things can run out. The powers that be are magicians. Like, *look here not there* type of thing.

They have conditioned us for who knows how many thousands of years. You might be asking ,as you should. - What can we do about it? - How can we resolve the above problem? - Can I change the world? YES, there is a simple yet seemingly complicated solution to bring peace to you, your loved ones and the rest of humanity. The whole book has subjects for all three things needed for eternal peace and prosperity which are:

1- **Body** - Physical mechanical and emotional.
2- **Mind** - Thinking.
3- **Soul**-Your higher SELF, the unseen that is present in you 24/7, or should I say that you are present inside the unseen and not the other way around.

One amazingly simple logical question destroys this fake deadly virus. If the virus is so deadly, then why were there no biohazard bins for the used masks and gloves? For over a year since the pandemic started, billions of used gloves and masks ended up in the regular garbage or in the seas and oceans. One more example, children under 2 years young do not have to wear a mask. Their immune system is supposed to be weaker than that of an adult, so how come no young children died from it. I don't know any child that has died from CONrona, do you? I thought so. Here's another example,

People that have a medical condition are not required to wear a mask. So, if a person already has a medical condition, wouldn't that make them a target for the monster called **CON**rona? I have a medical condition and I never wore a muzzle. The condition I have is called *"Critical thinking"*. The height of ignorance that our society has reached is shown on people being proud to have been injected by poison. They show pictures of their slave card online thinking they are virtuous, instead they are cowards that do not respect their own temple (body).

They do not innerstand that by being cowards, they will bury themselves alive and they could also pull down those that fight for the coward's freedom. First there were major forests fires which represent the lungs. Then the global virus attack the breathing of the lungs. Then a global broadcast scene of brutality where the victim cannot breathe was bombarding people's minds, and now people are chanting *"I can't breathe"*. Well, take off the mask if you cannot breath, simple as that.

If these are not alerts that it is time to practice breathworks, I don't know what is. We entered (or are in the transitioning period) the age of the Aquarius which astrologically is the air element. There is a lot more that can be written about this ridiculous lie of enormous proportions called CONrona.

A whole book about this subject would not be enough. Those that do not want us to live free and in peace are the real virus. Never in medical history has an annual disease (flu) completely disappeared to be replaced by another one with the exact same symptoms.

AFFIRMATIONS

- Viruses cannot exist in me.

- I only listen to my inner being.

- I don't fall for outside mind control schemes.

- I AM free of any external interference.

- I don't fall for low vibrational programs.

- I am not scared of anything

- I refuse to acknowledge any made-up tactics by

  illusionists.

4

NO NEED TO SUFFER

"Suffering and pain are always obligatory for a broad consciousness and a deep heart. Truly a great man, I think, must feel great sorrow in this world." - Fyodor Dostoevsky

Anyone can agree or disagree with the above statement. Any quote can be interpreted differently based on the consciousness or the times that we were or are living in now. Personally, I agree that struggling is required for growth and lessons, but suffering is not necessarily a requirement. Suffering is a requirement for people that lack knowledge and inner standing. What suffering means for someone, it can be considered struggling for someone else. Everyone has a different compass level.

A lesson can be repeated enough times until it is learned, which from the first time of the lessons to the last time, it could become a suffering. You suffer only if you keep repeating the same mistakes over and over.

Love can come without pain if you love yourself first. **"Pain is needed to enjoy freedom"**. It is because humans have been disconnected from their true selves and have been taught through wars and manipulation schemes that pain is needed for love and freedom.

When you wake up to the illusion and rediscover your true self, you will stop suffering because if there is a problem, you will fix the roots and not the leaves. He who doesn't know himself will keep repeating the same mistakes and therefore keep suffering and wasting time and energy fixing the leaves while the roots rot and there won't be any leaves or flowers to take care of anymore.

Afterwards, there will only be worms taking care of you. This is one of the interpretations based on the level of my consciousness. You can progress faster, without suffering when you see mistakes as lessons to be learned. I believe that in both ways you can progress, but progressing without suffering by knowing yourself first, you would achieve rapid progress because when the mind is clear and the heart is opened, life choices become healthier.

Become a determined person so you can live your life, instead of offering it to the otherworldly/dimensional entities. We are many and the greys are few. They *(the greys, aliens or whichever term you feel more comfortable asigning to otherworldly beings)* are indeed afraid of us. How can you recognize them? They are manipulative narcissists, with no feelings, no compassion, no responsibility, they suck your energy in any way they can, take advantage of you ... mostly in situations where they make you angry, jealous, fear etc.

They are finally leaving our **PLANE**t because the majority of people are becoming awake, although it may not seem so. The eye artwork (in the paperback version), represents the third eye (pineal gland) which metaphorically is crying from waiting to be opened/decalcified. A triangle pointing up is a symbol for male, the one pointing down represents the female. The powers behind the curtain have twisted and perverted the sacred symbols that represent the eternal beautiful human biology.

If you ask, what does the triangle and the one eye represent? They will tell you that those are illuminati signs. They are not. The Illuminati have hijacked your senses. As many know, the *otherwordly beings* are feeding from: fear, anger, jealousy, rage etc. When we consciously raise our vibration and frequency to a loving and happy frequency, they have no power over us. This is when they leave our space, so if you agree - work on your frequency every day and see the miracles happening in your life... Let suffering be a thing of the past.

The quality of your thoughts, words and actions will determine whether you will suffer or enjoy life. Either way, you will reach the destination. The only difference is that one of them will be a much longer path. You and only you, can determine how the movie (your life) ends. Will it end in disaster or in JOY and BLISS?

Be your own **AUTHOR**ity.
THERE IS NO NEED TO SUFFER .

5

BE A LEADER NOT A RULER

" It is the first responsibility of every citizen to question authority"
-Benjamin Franklin

You have been guided, or I should say misguided by different kinds of authorities since birth, but authorities nonetheless. Authorities such as your parents, teachers, and the media. Do you know who Medea is? MEDEA is the Greek goddess of illusion. She is also a witch (Footnote#2). Medea = MEDIA, right under your nose.

What does media(tv) do to people? It injects illusion of freedom, conditioning and indoctrination. I don't force my children to learn something, for example drawing or playing a musical instrument.

I can enforce, and the child may become good at that particular art, but it wouldn't be freely chosen. I would be an authority just as any other. By letting him/herself choose, the child also practices freedom and creativity. Many children studied certain things because their parents wanted them to. They ended up not loving or wanting to do it. Not always though, many times parents are right at guiding the children to choose the right things to learn, but eventually it has to be the child who chooses for himself.

> Parents pressure their children to succeed, because it's how they were conditioned by their parents and society. You can be successful in certain areas that bring you joy and happiness. Certain professions are good at making a better society, but most professions are based on an economical system that promotes selfishness, division and destruction.

What is different this time around, with a silent, yet tyrannical organization's quest to control humanity? They override the sovereign rights and the will of the people, who choose to follow what they know within themselves which is the appropriate thing to do for their families. The game that is being played out in marketplaces throughout the world , is much like it has always been. People in power seek out those who can be controlled by fear and propaganda.

> *Those who will not seek the truth, blindly follow the given narrative.*
> *That makes them allies to a plan they do not innerstand.*

History has seen it many times. The days of Church rule, when the high priest and king were often the same person. His word became law, and if you dared to disagree, the result was you were branded a heretic, an enemy of the state. Death was your punishment. Followers of the tyrant ruler would seek out those who disagreed or disobeyed. Millions died for their truth. Adolf Hitler initially pretended to be a man of the people. Until he could assemble an army of followers, who paid allegiance to him and his mission.

They watched and they worked, helping him with the extermination of many people. By taking away their sovereign rights, whether by weapon or by fear, he gained control. He too had sympathizers, who would seek out those who wanted only their rights to be free. Take a hard look around you right now, and what do you see?

I see a group of people that are putting every effort into removing the very God given sovereign rights of choice. The most basic right of keeping your body healthy and free. They have found allegiance in those who live in fear. Fear was so great that they would poison their own bodies at the demand of the ruling class. To make sure their actions were seen as benevolent, they insisted entire countries do the same thing.

> *Disobedience is mandatory when your basic rights are infringed upon.*

I have disobeyed the so-called man-made law hundreds of times during Korona (not the beer brand-K is not a typo) which was blown out of proportion and every time I disobeyed; I was being freed a little more. It is considered disobedience from the controllers' viewpoint. From my viewpoint and those that think and feel alike, it is considered obedience to our sovereign rights. We are sovereign beings by default.

What I and many others were doing was moral. Moral in the convenience of society as a whole. Regardless of what those that obeyed the man-made laws think or believe. Those that believe and follow immoral laws, deep down also want to be free. They are just on a level that they have not innerstood yet, which is the beauty of being free. We all are brothers and sisters. Some of us wake up earlier than others. Critical thinkers' beliefs bloom from the heart.

> *The beliefs of those that obey the immoral laws spring from the virus implanted in them by those that want society to be obedient and docile.*

Be your own authority. There are two kinds of people:

> *1- Those that will do what they are told, no matter what is right.*

> *2-Those that will do what is right, no matter what they are told.*

Which one are you?

AFFIRMATIONS:

- I AM my own authority.

- I do not take orders from anyone outside of myself.

- I AM powerful and willing to defend my sovereign rights.

- Freedom from tyranny is a must and I will not kneel.

- I will be an authority figure to my children, as a leader and not as a ruler.

- I AM the leader of my tribe.

Empty your mind. Fill it with wonder and exploration.

Unload the baggage of a lifetime you've been constantly carrying. It doesn't serve you. It only contributes to your self destruction. Unload the memories of the past that don't exist. Refuse to load wishful unknown future outcomes that you have created in your mind as a result of ignoring the present moment. If you don't want to be eaten by worms and ants, you better develop the ability to see things from an eagle's perspective.

Look beyond the invisible barriers that you have created. Work on your character and do not worry about your reputation. Your character is who you are, and your reputation is who people think you are.

6

CLEAR YOUR MIND AND BREAK FREE

"Your mind is your home, if you have a messy home you will trip, if it is tidied up you will walk with ease and flow like a river. You have two choices; to self-destruct or to expand" -Saimir Kercanaj

When your mind is calm, you can perceive everything beautifully. A troubled mind is like dirty water, if you stir the water it will stay dirty. If you don't mess with the water, it will clear itself up. It is the same with your mind. Let things go. Don't over think. Observe with no judgement and you will see how your mind will become clear. Most of your stress comes from the way you respond, not the way life is. Life is how you perceive it to be. You perceive it with your mind, and your thoughts trigger emotions. Change the way you see the outside world and your inside universe will change based on your new adjustments.

Find positives in any situation. Every situation has both negative and positive sides to it. It is up to you to decide if you are aiming for a temporary solution (Band-Aid), or a long-lasting solution (healing). It all depends on you. Nobody will come to save you, but YOU.

I know Christ Consciousness, not Jesus Christ the person that religious people think of, but the ideology, the inner love frequency . The love and light that we have inside. We are born with it. Care, love, compassion, forgiveness etc, are by default in us. Also greed, lie, deceit, selfishness etc, are by default in us as well. We are both good and evil. It's just energy. Two sides of the same coin. Yin/Yang, light/darkness, black/white wolf. Depending on which one you feed the most - The black or the white wolf, Light or Darkness.

Both (white/dark) are needed to be "whole". There needs to be a balance between light and dark. Years ago, I was constantly perceiving the outside world as a disaster, and I was suffering inside by blaming people and situations. That was nobody's fault but mine. I was an angry person and couldn't understand why. I was getting mad at everything and everyone until I realized that all my emotions had to do with the way I was responding to the perception I had of the outside world.

Little at a time I was rebuilding myself, or should I say, I realized I had to start dropping the weight that I had accumulated as a result of my misinterpretation of the outside world. As an angry person I was only hurting myself. As a saying goes:

> "Holding on to anger is like grasping a hot coal with the intent of throwing it at someone else, but you will be the only one that gets burned"

The external world is a projection from within the mind, you will live most of your life in your head (mentally), so make sure it is a nice place to be. It is your garden. Water it, nurture it or else it will wither. You are your own obstacle.

> Move your ego away and be guided by your higher SELF, the one you were meant to be. The one it was, is and will always be within you.

Many people throughout my life tell me they are bored at home, or on their days off. This boggles my mind. You are free at home and can do anything you want. Home is your castle. Make home your vacation. People that can't wait to go on vacation are the ones that live in hell (metaphorically). With the exception of those that go on vacation to explore different cultures and learn. When you go on vacation to get away from your everyday messy life, you will only be happy temporarily, and when you get back nothing has changed, and it can be even worse because of your illusionary temporary happiness.

IT'S ALL IN YOUR HEAD.

If you stop comparing your lifestyle with others, then you will appreciate what you have. You will innerstand that you are the key to your happiness and your mind will be clear of all the society's enforced conditioned congestion. When the mind is clear, you will make healthy choices and you will realize that happiness was nowhere else but inside of you.

Many people have knowledge of things but don't know how to apply the knowledge for the betterment of their mental and physical and psyche health.

There is also that demographic of people that have a will and a purpose in life but don't have knowledge or don't know how to properly apply it.

Loading your brain with knowledge and not using it properly or not using it at all will only clutter it. The first step is to get rid of the garbage accumulated in your mind throughout your life. You also have to add healthy thinking/lifestyle or else you will not grow. When you get rid of negative thoughts, emotions or habits, I suggest you do it one at a time. Your brain will overload if you overwhelm yourself with doing more than one thing at a time, since you have fallen from comfort to a certain degree. After a week you do one change, the next week introduce the new thing to change while continuing the first thing you started to change and so on. The same way you were loaded with bad stuff gradually, the same way you will undo those things gradually.

When I was researching about eating healthy, I stopped consuming everything I thought was negative such as meat consumption, sugar etc., and I was getting sick. It's like withdrawal. Technically I was not getting sick, it was the reaction of my body. A shake up was happening. Do you know why they don't write in cursive anymore? At least one of the reasons that I can think of is to separate us. How so?

Everything you say, read or write gets recorded into your subconscious. Anything repeated enough times, becomes the primary way of expressing ourselves. Writing in separated/disconnected letters (as opposed to cursive writing), bombards us subconsciously about being separated and not united. Never underestimate the power of the subconscious mind. When you have a clear mind and heart you are a fortress that nobody can penetrate from the outside.

The only person that can damage your auric fortress is "you" from the inside. You can be your own worst enemy. Overthinking creates a disorganized mind. While in the process of writing this book I stopped a few times for a few months at a time, why? Overthinking for stupid reasons. Thinking that maybe the place that runs the self-publishing business would close, or that the manuscript file of the book might get corrupted, or that something might happen by the time I finish it and many other delusional thinking on my part. That's not healthy thinking.

My mind was disorganized. Now that I'm thinking straight, I can think of a few reasons why the overthinking happened. At that time I was not in a healthy state or mind by trying to do too many things at once. Secondly, it was the first time that I was writing a book, which was a huge task for me.

Another reason was like when I draw or paint, I don't just do a rough sketch and then later add details. I start perfecting right away. Same thing for the writing of this book. Most, if not all other authors just write down a rough manuscript, then later on fix the grammatical errors, sentence construction etc.

I started fixing the grammar right away (to the best of my ability) and sentences, page set up construction etc. Maybe this was the reason I got overwhelmed. I'm a perfectionist, at least I'd like to think I am. I'm using this term loosely, but it means I try to do things the best possible way that I can handle.

Another reason is that there is a time and place for everything. Some things need to stop being done to just continue at a later time. You wouldn't enforce a baby to run that just learned how to crawl. First the baby will crawl, then walk and then learn how to run.

My point is, in order to organize your brain sometimes, you don't have to do many things. By not doing them at all is enough for the brain to breathe until the brain is ready to operate efficiently. Your body can fix itself by deep breathing, so does your brain can fix itself if you don't overwhelm it with worries and fears. The opposite is equally important true, meaning to do things in order to organize your brain.

The difference is that doing physical/mental exercises for the betterment of your mental health is only good when anything you do, you do it with pleasure and with passion.

This is only possible when your heart and its 40 thousand neurons are involved. Don't be caught in "time". Time is just an illusion . If your heart is open, then the mind becomes your heart's best friend.

My favorite quote of all time that made me realize the first big step to growth, was philosopher Socrates' quote:

"I AM intelligent because I know that I know nothing".

I heard this quote before but didn't innerstand it because I was drowning in a deep sea of distorted thoughts and beliefs that were acquired from a whole lifetime of opinions from others. Especially when it has to do with religious beliefs. The Bible or any other religious text talking about God, is not about what/who created everything.

The Bible and the other texts talk about the super intelligent species that created our human species on Earth. That's why we are made in the image of god. I used a small g on purpose. Those that created us are not the real God (whatever God means to you). Yes, we are the pinnacle of creation when we unleash our full potential. Religion and other schemes imposed by the controllers have hindered our ability to unlock that power. All religious texts and buildings are loaded with satanic symbolism.

You want to find God? Look within your heart and not in your blurry mind. My intention is to make people aware of their potential when the mind is free of noise. I was struggling to create the perfect title for this book. One night in May of 2021 after meditating, I went to bed and started lucid dreaming unintentionally. My mind had questions about which title should be the right one. And there it was , the title became known to me.

My bet is that it was my higher self that projected the title. The Higher Self is perfect (almost?). It's not confused like we are when in a regular conscious state. The being that showed me the book title could have been one or a group of entities or interdimensional other worldly ETs. The Church/Mosque teaches that otherwordly beings (that you may see while meditating) are demons/jinns.

Yes, there are demons but only when you are a hostage of beliefs. If you believe that there is a Hell, then your consciousness will attract those low energy malevolent entities when you are conscious every day, or while you dream, astral travel or lucid dream.

I am only writting down my thoughts here. You may have lucid dreams or not. If you haven't, then you are in for a good treat. Looking within, I discovered myself, the real me and not the one I was told to be.

Only after I cleared my mind and opened my heart. You cannot have a clear mind if you have fallen for the thousands of years old scheme called: Religion. I mean organized religion. All religions have many truths in them. The problem is that they have been infiltrated by higher powers (dark forces) and manipulated so that those that follow religion, are always confused. A confused population can be easily **CON***trolled*.

Get out of your head, leave the noises (opinions/beliefs) behind.

~~~~~

"When you have access to knowledge but you don't use/practice it, that makes you a dangerous person to society" - S.K

You, me, or anyone else, can interpret knowledge differently. All of us are different on an individual conscious level, although those that resonate with each other may seem the same, they still are on a slightly different level/frequency. Since words (and the energy that they carry) create your reality, you may just simply speak (what you know) to people and you may ruin some and uplift others.

Those that will be uplifted are the ones that are open minded. Those that have already been through the first level of awakening from within, will question everything. Those that can be ruined are those that are confused and have not realized their true purpose yet. Therefore, it is very important that you stay silent if you don't know how your words will affect you or someone else.

Two kinds of dangerous people
can bring suffering in the world.

1- Those that have no empathy
and use knowledge to destroy

2- Those that have a good heart/empathy
but by being naive/ignorant of their own
powers, they destroy themselves and
contribute in the destruction of society.

Which one are you?
The builder or the destroyer?

If you know that you speak with confidence, then go ahead and spread knowledge even though some may be triggered by it. In that case, it is good because you are helping them to begin their healing journey. Anything that triggers you means that you are not fully healed. When you speak your knowledge with confidence it means that you have converted that knowledge into wisdom. That's what wisdom is, "**knowledge acquired, practiced and mastered**".

Silence is the best tool to not create havoc into your and other people lives. Do not get confused when your words create havoc in someone's mental/emotional state of being when your knowledge is wisdom. Their so called "*havoc mental state*" is simply their shadow that they must face. Everyone must face their own shadow. You cannot run from it. Try running from your shadow on a sunny day. Good luck escaping it.

7

ORGANIZED RELIGION

"Religion is like a blind man looking in a black room for a black cat that isn't there, and finding it"-Oscar Wilde

"Religion is like a pair of shoes, find one that fits for you but don't make me wear your shoes." - George Carlin

Religion is the beLIEf in someone else's experience. Spirituality is having your own experience. What you believe in, doesn't make you a free thinker. The ability to change your beliefs when you are presented with new information does. I always hear people referring to God as "he". Many have fallen for the lie that God is a man up there in the sky. Many people of Christian belief have told me that if I don't believe everything in the Bible, then I don't believe any of what is written in it. Yet when I speak of omnipresence and inseparable nature that is, they are lost.

When I ask if they believe they could do the same work as Jesus did, they change the subject because they don't want to deal with it. It requires effort, discipline, pure unconditional love to ascend and become all of those things that Jesus talked about (regardless if a physical person named "Jesus or Jeshua or whatever" existed or not). The message is important not names and dates. His-story is manipulated just as "time" is.

The Bible has created more confusion, wars, hatred, racism than any other document in the history of the world. If you cannot contain yourself enough to not rape, pillage and murder, what good is a book going to do, except that it will produce more guilt, like it has for many people. If you need a book to produce humility, kindness, compassion and love, then you are already lost, because you are not doing it out of natural expression, but one driven by fear of the afterlife. The Bible is a fairytale when read literally. It is what church teaches people, the literal sense which does not make sense.

The bible story is an allegory. It is very cryptic and truthful even after being edited many times. It is still full of truth that the church does not teach people. The bible teaches you how to meet your maker, which is within you. Only those that have a mind to make sense of it will decipher it.

The rest of the people will be lost and have no idea what life is, and who God is. Do you think that if they used the word "consciousness" in the Bible, people would innerstand? Of course not.

The phrase "mother, father and son" means "The Holy Trinity". Christianity suppresses the feminine aspect by replacing the "Mother" with the Holy Spirit (e-motional **innerG**=Emotional Energy), which is the feminine aspect of spiritual essence. Christians: Father-Son-Holy spirit Jewish: Kether-Chokmah-Binah Hindu: Brahma-Vishnu-Shiva Egyptian: Osiris-Horus-Isis.

Soul energy is the masculine aspect dealing with intellect. The child is the physical body when learns to navigate the physical realms with spirit and soul as guides. Separate but equal-The trinity is what so many refer to as "God". No book (Bible/Koran or any other religious book) can tell you what God wrote. The human brain is the world's greatest computer because it is self-aware, self-thinking, self-learning, and can even reprogram itself.

> *Why would God implant such great abilities into our heads and then give us religions that discourages intelligent critical thinking in exchange for blind dumb faith? Also, the theory (made up) of God rewarding good deeds with 72 virgins is both morally and logically unacceptable. God can't reward good deeds with women. Women are not subjects. This is from a patriarcal only mindset that suppresses women/feminine. Without strong women, men are easily swayed away and controlled, especially by being sent to wars fighting an imaginary enemy.*

Look within so you can have a clear mind and an open heart, instead of looking for answers externally from those that want to keep you suppressed and dumb. Religion (all of them) will never reform mankind because religion is slavery. Many religious people that believe in Jesus (as in the physical person portrayed by church and not as in the Christ consciousness) would disagree with this, but they do not know that Jesus hated religion. He knew that religion was/is slavery. Clear your mind of the man-made be**LIE**fs. Mike Hermann hit the nail on the head with the quote:

> *"Organized religion is like organized crime; It preys on people's weakness, generates huge profits for its operators and is almost impossible to eradicate".*

It is almost impossible, until you realize that Christ (Christ consciousness=The highest vibration which is unconditional love) is within. When Jesus *(regardless of if he actually existed or not)* said that he was coming back, he meant Christ consciousness was, the energy of the soul fully connected to the divine through the human heart.

We have to bring that high vibrational consciousness back through our own lives. Not through someone else's words. People took his words literally and it has confused humanity to this day. Go within. Have an intimate relationship with your inner self and bring out the Christ Consciousness from within.

Anyone or anything outside of you must not be worshipped. A God that threatens you with hell, disease and suffering for you to recognize that supposed entity as God, is nothing but a man-made scarecrow. You either have a brain or you don't. You can't say that God is the most intelligent being who gave you a brain and at the same time not using your brain. No real God would need validation from his children, only a fictional one would. A fictional God as in an idea/ideology, or a physical one that pretends to be a God for the purpose to control people through fear and suffering. There are no external forces/entities called "God" or " Satan" controlling us.

Good and evil are our own spiritual awareness or the lack of it. There are only a group or groups of *beings* lurking in the dark that have managed to convince/condition people that people are small, powerless and that they need to believe in outside forces. The terms God and Satan are made up. Even though different people have a different understanding of these terms. I too, use the term God sometimes, but in my case what I know (I don't believe, I KNOW) this term means is described at the beginning of this chapter. When you transcend duality you will realise that God and Satan are the same entity, YOU. You are both God and Satan, you are both the builder and the destroyer, you are both the cause and the effect, you are both the poison and the remedy, you are both Adam and Eve.

In the book *YOU ARE THE ONE* by *Pine G. Land* the author writes:

> *"Adam is an Atom. Eve is an Electron. The story is mythology based on life beginning with "Splitting the Atom", as electrons are the 'rib' of the Atom. God is the 'Good' of your higher mind, the Cerebrum. Devil is the 'Evil' of your lower mind, the Cerebellum. Heaven is your 'Head', the highest 'heaved' up place of your body and higher nature. Hell is your 'Heel', the lowest place of your body and lower nature. The snake is electromagnetic energy. The tree is your spine. The apple is consciousness. Kundalini energy means activating your pineal gland; hence, conquering your dragon."*

One of my all time favourite truther/comedians George Carlin had this to say about religion:

"Religion has convinced people that there's an invisible man living in the sky. Who watches everything you do every minute of every day. And the invisible man has a list of ten specific things he doesn't want you to do. And if you do any of these ten things, he will send you to a special place, of burning and fire and smoke and

torture and anguish for you to live forever, and suffer, and burn, and scream and cry, until the end of time...BUT HE LOVES YOU, he loves you and he neeeeeds MONEY."

Here is the original YouTube 10 minute clip of George Carlin's speech on religion. https://www.youtube.com/watch?v=8r-e2NDSTuE

It is clear that all this suffering and burning in hell idea was implanted in the minds of the masses for the purpose of control. Speaking of money, do you think God needs money? God is all wise, all powerful, all knowing, God does not need any money. Money is man-made, money is not evil in itself, even though many people think that money is the root of all evil. Ignorance is the root of all evil. Money is just a means of communication, just as this book or any other book or a cellphone are a form of communication. We, individually decide how we use all forms of communication. Do we use them to love, care and help one another, or do we use them to destroy and harm ourselves and others?

What God means to me and some others, may mean something else to a huge group of people/beings. The only difference between the two different innerstanding/understanding of the word/term "God" lies in the difference between beLIEving *(external forces, people, ideologies)* or kNOWing *(understanding from within, knowing that we are little Gods, materialized extensions of the Great Spirit, or little Satans if we stray off the righteous path).*

8

UNCLUTTER YOUR BAGGAGE

"My dear friend, clear your mind of "CAN'T" -Samuel Johnson

The beauty of life is that we all have different opinions. It would be a boring life if we all thought the same. Although we may not agree with each other in some opinions, in a different lifetime (past or future life) or timeline (alternate dimensional) we do agree. That is what has made our world and the universe progress, our different ideas and perceptions from this lifetime, past lifetimes (lives) and alternate timelines. Multiply the billions of opinions of this life with billions of opinions of past lives plus billions of perspectives of billions of alternate timelines, also adding future timelines and you see that we have an infinite number of possibilities and probabilities.

The above section might give a bit of a headache to some, but it is necessary to innerstand and clear your mind. First, you must be aware of what it is that has cluttered it in the first place. The clutter is *"thoughts, memories and expectations"*. A cluttered mind does not necessarily mean that it is loaded with bad stuff. It can also mean that it is disorganized.

When you organize your thoughts and feelings, you are the master of your Godself and the relation of yourself with the universe will be in unison and coherent. Your best ideas can come when you go for a jog, or when you take a bath, or when you read. You will almost never have ideas when you are brainstorming in an office, or in a group setting.

For inspiration and creativity, seek silence and a clear mind, not pressure, or external noise. Seek solitude and the answers will come. Only with a clear mind will you find the answers. Do not insist on defending your beliefs when you are presented with someone else's viewpoint.

The enormously powerful and stupid have one thing in common. They do not alter their views to fit the facts. They alter the facts to fit their views.

The word "can't", should not exist in your mind. Nothing is impossible. We all get inspired by each other one way or another. Only a stone may not get inspired, but this is debatable. There is one kind of stone that has a consciousness. That stone is a diamond. The diamond is associated with activating the seventh chakra which is the crown chakra Sahasrara.

Uniting the mind with the body. While the diamond is regarded as the strongest precious stone, it is also regarded as a stone of immense exceptional power because it is capable of reaching into us and opening spiritual doors. It is said that diamonds represent truth. Overthinking is detrimental to your mental health. As the 6th century philosopher Seng-ts'an said : *"When love and hate are both absent, everything becomes clear and undisguised. Make the smallest distinction, however, and heaven and earth are set infinitely apart".*

You must be blind and deaf to see clearer. Your mind is polluted by images and sounds of those that do not know you, and other things that don't serve in your developmental progression. You must unclutter your beautiful mind.

AFFIRMATIONS

- I AM deaf, I AM blind.
- I AM free with a clear mind.
- I observe and let it be.
- I have no choice but to be me.
- I AM happy, and I AM free.
- I AM part of this beautiful game.
- I AM life, and that's the game's name.

9

BE HAPPY FOR OTHERS' HAPPINESS

"You are happy when you help others become happy"

-Dalai Lama

T hroughout my life I have seen people enjoy the sadness of someone that they don't like, rather than focusing on their own happiness. The truth is that those people do not know what happiness is. When you know what happiness is, you would want others to experience it too. Let me make a recent example. Eventually all our debts will be zeroed, because they are illegal. It is a debt out of thin air. A debt that is not based on precious metals such as gold, silver, copper, palladium etc.

Some debts were forgiven in 2020 as a test of the new quantum system . One person was mad about one woman's house debt being forgiven. This mad person said that it wasn't fair that she worked all her life and paid all her mortgage. Mortgage from Latin means "pledge to death". I am telling you that you should be happy when other people's debts get forgiven.

Yours will too, eventually. If you release happiness energy you will get that back. If you are not happy with another person, you are telling the universe/ God that you do not agree with creation, with the order of things. Therefore, based on the law of attraction you will get back what you give which is disapproval, hate and lack of abundance. You reap what you sow. Some need material riches to be happy, while some others know that happiness is free.

There are two trips you need to take to find happiness and a perfect life: The unlimited kilometer trip to find the perfect life, or the zero distance one to find the happiness within.

I know which one I choose, the zero distance one. Which path are you choosing? Stay away from toxic people. Be around the light bringers, the magic makers, the world shifters. They challenge, uplift and expand you. Those heartbeats (light bringers) are your family. That family is your tribe. Be happy for others.

> You need nature, you need magic. You need adventure. You need freedom and truth. You need stillness. You do not need any more sleep (metaphorically), you need to wake up and live.

Be a member of the tribe. In this society we cannot thrive unless we love each other unconditionally. Any perception you have of someone, is a reflection of you. If you are happy for others, you are happy. If you are unhappy for others, you will not be happy about yourself either. Be happy by focusing and enjoying what you have, instead of being unhappy by focusing on what you don't have.

Reflect onto the world,
what you would love the world
to reflect back onto you.

10

BE YOURSELF, EVERYONE ELSE IS TAKEN

"Don't change so people will like you, be yourself and the right people will love the real you" -Unknown

Many people do not know who they are, therefore they will try to impersonate other people to make them feel important. Do not worry about others, be yourself and improve on it every day. Pretending to feel good when you don't or faking positivity and confidence at work or anywhere else, drains your energy and increases your risk of burnout.

Picture a glass half filled with water, what do you think it is, half full or half empty? I say there are three choices. Half full, half empty and full. The full glass has 50% water and 50% air. Which one you are, depends on the quality of your thoughts and actions. Relying on others to teach you, will only add more strain in your wholeness.

You cannot get educated by this decayed system in which people study to pass exams, and teach others to pass exams, but nobody knows anything. You learn something by doing it yourself, by experimenting.

Do what needs to be done and not what you want to do. If you are only a taker, you break the law of dynamic exchange. You must also give. Being great is not measured by money or status, but by courage to be yourself and opening your heart to unconditional love. Anyone that has ever hurt you, should have taught you discernment .

I have met people online that have innerstood me better than those that have known me all my life. Be yourself and you do not need anyone else to save you. You do not need aliens to come and save you. They may watch over us and guide us when we are too stubborn to see the truth we refuse to accept.

We are growing now to the point that we can take care of ourselves. You innerstand that, right ?

You have the power within you to believe in yourself. Accept yourself, love yourself. Be your own savior. If anyone is going to change the world, it needs to begin with a good hard look in the mirror and making healthy choices.

It is not hard, it's like...say the mirror is fogged up, it's still the same mirror. Wipe the fog away and there is your beautiful soul.

Love it and get your hands dirty by wiping the mirror so you can see clarity. Never let anyone tell you that you cannot do something. Stay positive. Treat your fellow brothers and sisters with love and respect. Do not waste time with negative people who think you are crazy because of your beliefs

Never allow yourself to start your day in a bad mood. That kind of bacterial thought will grow like a fungus, and it is contagious. Do not sweat the small stuff. Too many people waste their time and energy on stuff that is out of their control. Keep smiling and make others smile. We are all here with a purpose, it's up to us to figure it out. Pray, meditate and keep your mind free of all the useless clutter.

Make a list of 5 nice things you want to do tomorrow. Start with some easy tasks and then challenge yourself once you get the hang of it. Practice loving yourself and others. You may feel overlooked, rejected and ignored by the people who are not meant to be in your life. Let them go in peace. You can only be yourself, everyone else is taken.

Look ahead in gratitude and do not fall for this distorted reality "Matrix".

11

ARE WE IN THE 10010110?

D o you think the air you breathe is real? Or the food you eat? Or things / people you touch or interact with? What is real? Morpheus from the movie (documentary) MATRIX said it best.

> *"What is real? How do you define real? If you are talking about what you can feel, what you can smell, what you can taste and see. Then real is simply electrical signals interpreted by your brain. The Matrix is everywhere. It is all around us. Even now, in this very room. You can see it when you look out of the window, or when you turn on the tell-lie-vision/ TV. You can feel it when you go to work, when you go to church, when you pay your taxes. It is the world that has been pulled over your eyes to blind you from the truth. You are a slave Neo (NEO = "new" in Greek). Like everyone else you were born into bondage, born into a prison that you cannot smell or taste or touch. A prison for your mind."*

Neo is also an anagram for "One". We all have a script to follow, a script by the Universe, or the Creator. A randomized script that may look like we are operating based on our free will, but a script, nonetheless. Or not ? Evil forces have been controlling the Earth for a long time. These undivine entities that have deserted light, know and innerstand the order of things. They know how to manipulate your mind.

If you think your thoughts are yours, think again. There is a good chance that your thoughts are not even stored in your brain. The brain is just an organ, a tool for thoughts. A secondary hard drive. The master hard drive exists in the unseen, the ether, the quantum field. I suggest you watch the 2010 movie "INCEPTION". A thought is injected into you subconsciously in the form of images , numbers, colors, words or sounds. I am talking when the evil or the powers that be, have an agenda to impose on you, not when you genuinely think for yourself. We will find out if it is possible or not. I already know and innerstand the answer.

You will too. I AM going to write an analogy about evil controlling humanity. Picture an ant on a tiled floor, the ant cannot easily find the exit because there are many crisscross lines in the tiles, but we humans being high from above, can easily see the exit. Same with us humans, we are very disoriented with our everyday busy life. Distractions and division between us through nationality, gender, color of the skin, social status etc. The controllers can easily see the order of things.

They know the exit. They have made sure that we are so overwhelmed with the corrupted and distracted system (tiled floor), that we are not able to see the exit which is remarkably close to us. By the end of this book, you should and will realize the exit and be surprised that it was so obvious and easy yet has been hidden right in front of your very own eyes. Based on the Universal Law of respecting "free will", the Elites have to tell us what they are going to do, through books, movies, music videos, and TV shows before they do it. Otherwise, their enslavement plan would not work.

It is a CHAOS MAGIC that they always predicated around the HEGELIAN DIALECTIC-Problem/Reaction/Solution. The twin tower collapse was already predicted through shows, card games and more. The supposed Corona virus was also predicted through a book of over 30 years ago and through movies of the last decade, also through the videogame Resident Evil. If we do not innerstand the hidden messages and sigils, then it is our fault, not theirs. We stay entertained and distracted while thinking it's just a movie, or just a book. Meanwhile they create all the fear and propaganda through many different deceptive ways, and we willingly provide them with 'loosh'. Loosh is the energy that they extract from us by being in fear, anxiety, worries and suffering.

The events that they tell us in advance are not really predictions but more like planned predictions. They tell us sneakingly in advance, so they mitigate their karma. Karma is what they believe in. Once you wake up from this false electromagnetic web of energy or matrix created by them, you will realize that you are not in your body. Your body is in you. You are not in your mind; your mind is in you. You are not in the universe; the universe is in you. You have been conditioned to think that you are small, that you are useless, that you have no worth, that you are nobody.

The truth is that you are the universe, you are a heavenly being. Say: " NO MORE " being the provider of your life force's energy to the distorted reality created by those that want you to be forever slaves.

My genuine intention from the heart is to make you aware so you can free your mind. I can only show you the path. You are the one that has to walk it. Nobody should infringe on your free will. You can escape the Matrix and you can escape this worldwide deceit .

If you want to have success in escaping it, then you must stop watching tell-LIE-vision a.k.a. TV, because the device itself, besides the mind control programs that projects in your mind, also releases a harmful EMF-Electromagnetic field that bombards your psyche constantly.

Stop believing in mainstream media or traditions. False beliefs can create a distortion of your perception of the world and anything within and around it. Stop eating processed junk food because they are designed to keep your body in an acidic state which makes it prone to disease.

Stop going to clubs or parties as you will be courted by low vibrational spirits such as alcohol and other drinks that are created with the sole purpose to keep your vibration low.

That way you cannot think clearly because then another entity can easily possess you while you are under alcohol influence, and the sounds that are played in clubs or parties vibrate in disharmony with your biological harmonious body. I never heard Mozart in a club or party where alcohol was the main offering of fake pleasure.

Classical music and alcohol do not match. The classical music tune derives from the center of the universe. Its harmonious frequency is designed to be in harmony with the frequency of love that all of us are embedded to. I AM talking about parties where distortion of Light/false reality is involved such as alcohol, lifeless food, disharmonious music, one night stands etc. Do not watch adult content as it will damage your gray matter in the brain. By regularly watching that kind of *immoral content* it distances you from reality and you will be addicted to a fantasy. Not only that, but it can even damage the relationship you have with your partner. The desire to get rid of the addictions is a desire in itself.

So, not to be overwhelmed and discouraged, get rid of one addiction at a time. The above addictions were some examples. Anything can be an addiction. Be aware and realize your own addictions and work on eliminating them one at a time. Mine is buying books. I promised myself that as soon as this book is released, I will not buy 10-15 books a month anymore. I will cut it down to just 9. No, but seriously I have this addiction, especially in the 1st half of 2021when I met my friend JJ (Jason) online . He is a an extreme book addict.

Thanks to my association with him, I have now a big library home. All the negative low vibrational activities I mentioned previously and a lot more, are designed to separate you from the source which is in the center of your heart. It is where God rests, waiting for you to acknowledge it and be finally ONE with the source. The only thing keeping this matrix alive is our ignorance. The distorted reality or matrix that we are part of cannot exist in love. It is built on lies, hence the term " distorted". Before adding positive behavior and loving feelings to this beautiful world, you must get rid of those things that imprisoned you in the first place.

First you must be aware of the existence of problems before getting rid of them. Question everything and everyone, search for the truth. I cannot tell you what your truth is. Only you have the power to realize it. In this book the truth is in your face. By the end of the book you should realize the truth. I am not saying it because you must realize it yourself.

If I tell you, then I hinder your natural ability to discern. I have purposefully encoded quite a few words in a certain way to make you realize the truth. Do not get discouraged if you do not realize it. You may realize it if you read the book more than once, or you might realize it at a later date. Everyone is at a different level. Certain things must be learned first before moving on to the next. I, myself, have innerstood the meaning of certain books months later when I have reread them.

The first time you read something you may not get it, and that is fine. You cannot go to the 2nd floor unless you go through the first floor first. If you practice the affirmations and meditations , it is guaranteed that you will inner stand the truth. I mean you will feel the truth. I tell you this because I can confirm it. I went through dark periods in my life to realize THE truth.

I can guarantee that you can escape the matrix by letting go of the weight that is keeping you down and you will fly if you practice affirmations, mindfulness, meditating daily and of course by inner standing this book and other similar books that promote critical thinking.

I purposefully touch on many different subjects that are a part of the same reality that we are trying to break free from. I didn't want to write a book where a specific subject would go on for 30-40 pages. Some chapters have to do with the negative part of being in the matrix, and with the solution of how to get out of the matrix. Many have fallen prey to the traps of the matrix placed by the master magician mind controllers. Go out in nature, start meditating, work on yourself, realize the true nature of who you really are.

Practice gratitude, compassion and the matrix will fall in no time, as it is already falling. If the Matrix keeps staying alive, so will the suffering and the struggle that humans will have to keep enduring. Our fear, anxiety, panicking and worries keep the matrix alive. We are living in extraordinary times. We are witnessing the shift of the ages.

> The financial system will restructure itself. The Matrix is falling apart, and a new society will be born. Our current reality is shifting, and changes will affect everyone. Imagine that there is another positive loving civilization beyond our current dimension/reality.

They (other civilizations) are willing to contact humanity and are assisting us to achieve world peace which will result in ending poverty and hunger. They are helping us create a fair and transparent new financial system, bringing justice back again and replacing the corrupt legal, political and banking system, assisting us to heal the environment, save rainforests and animal species, and to reveal new advanced technologies to humanity. Are you capable of escaping the 10010110 (Footnote#3)-Matrix?) No Matrix = Bliss, Love, Abundance, Light, Freedom, Peace, Unity, Cosmic aliveness everywhere . WAKE UP - THE Truth is calling, Yes, the MATRIX is falling.

AFFIRMATIONS:

Even if you do not believe you are capable of doing what these affirmations say, you must say them as if you do. Remember ? You must bombard yourself with positive uplifting loving words. Also, when you want to get rid of an addiction or any other negative emotions or thoughts that does not serve you, say the appropriate affirmation with conviction. You must reprogram your cells.

Your perception dictates your inner biology.

- I AM the Matrix destroyer.

- The Matrix is in its last days and new blissful life will spring.

- I let go of any addiction that is holding me back.

- I send Light and Love to everyone on Earth.

- I AM liberated from the trap that is called the " Matrix ".

- Life is sprouting from within, and Violet flame Light brightens my inner being and everyone surrounding me.

- I AM aligned with my higher self and with the divine order which Love reigns within every life form on Earth including animals, birds, plants, oceans and all life forms living in it.

12

BUILT AND SHATTERED BY THE ANUNNAKI

"Goodness, armed with power, is corrupted; and pure love without power is destroyed." -Reinhold Niebuhr

To realize who you are, you might need to know who you were, at least who you think you were. We are comprised of many fragments. In its original intended creation, we were whole. A long time ago a group of Extraterrestrials called the Anunnaki landed on Earth. That group's purpose was to mine gold because their planet's atmosphere was getting destroyed. Gold is a super conductive element and they needed it to save their planet's atmosphere. The Anunnaki are/were known to be ruthless rulers. They (most of them) have no respect for human life, and they infringed big time on our sovereign rights. Our species has been created many times before.

The Anunnaki used their own species' reptilian brain capability to use against us. The reason for that, (as far as it is known) is that we as a human species were developing our consciousness and the reptilians didn't want us to become smart.

They only wanted us to be able to take simple commands for digging gold. Our DNA had the other species' DNA. Those other species were benevolent ones that believed in the cosmic Law of One. As the story goes based on the personal translations of the Sumerian Tablets by Zecharia Sitchin, this group of Aliens called the Anunnaki crossed their DNA with that of Homo erectus in order to create mankind for the purpose of using humans as slaves to mine gold and other minerals.

Countless books have been written about the Anunnaki, so I AM going to simplify it and explain the point of this chapter's name.

There were two Anunnaki brothers (factions). The good brother and the rest of the benevolent ETs are the ones that crept into our DNA, the chakra system, the Goddess gift that is called "sexual energy" and the rest of what makes us whole. As per the story/legend, the evil brother wanted us to be slaves forever by relying on the genetic blueprint of the reptilian lower brain (fight or flight) that we have. Throughout thousands of years the good brother and his white brotherhood initiates were pushing us to develop and become intelligent species, while the evil brother and his minions have always infiltrated every brotherhood society that the good brother had created. It has always been a war between two factions of who will rule the Earth. Hence, we have the **Light vs Dark** term. I didn't mention the brothers' names because they are known under different names throughout history and different religions. It would cause more confusion than it already has.

Every single war in known history has been created by the reptilians (Draco's subspecies) for the purpose of control and power. Their main reason was and is to harvest our souls as they are soul rippers. They extract our energy called ' loosh'. This energy is extracted when we live in fear, are demoralized and are powerless.

> *All wars happened as a result of the Anunnaki's demands. Throughout history, they have infiltrated every single government institution and put their minions as public, political figures to supposedly represent 'WE THE PEOPLE'.*

It was always a lie, governments represented the interest of those blood suckers that they represented. They have always sacrificed people. In the old times those that represented the reptilians used to cut people's heads and do many other atrocious crimes so they could please their gods. In this case, the gods were the evil reptilians. I purposefully wrote gods with small 'g', because they are not the real God.

In modern times, the sacrifices are in the form of wars, vaccines , medical institutions and all kinds of legal drugs allowed by the same people that have an interest in the destruction of families and all life forms that vibrate in Love frequency.

There have been few exceptions throughout history where leaders of some countries had society's best interest in mind. You know what happened to those beautiful loving leaders? They were killed. Earlier I mentioned, the good brother and the White Brotherhood also want to rule Gaia or Earth. You might be wondering that if he and his Alliance want us to be free but at the same time want to rule the Earth, then how can they be good by wanting to rule in the first place? Think of it this way;

> *There are two fathers. One father wants to rule his wife and kids for personal gain and power by teaching his family lies, hate, deceit, selfishness etc. While the other father wants to rule his wife and children by teaching them love, care, compassion, gratitude, freedom, peace etc.*

See? They both want to rule. One's intention is to create destruction, while the other wants to create wholeness/unity. "**Ruling**" is a poor word to use in the case of the good father. The better world would be "**leading**". As it has been proven, we humans need to be led. Not singularly, but as a whole. We were and are like sheep that wander in all directions. Many, if not most people cannot fathom it is possible to be led by good people.

Yes, it is possible. Only when we are true to ourselves. Only then can we build a WHOLE, healthy society. When other people don't like what you say or do, by being true to yourself , a new piece of the real you surfaces. In this life you are doing your part and being part of the glue that rebuilds the fragmented society. I have seen many people that have worked within themselves and innerstood the true meaning of life.

The number is growing. You are reading this book, and that makes you part of the glue that is bringing our true-life essence on the surface, so the rest of the civilization can become free. Are other civilizations ET (Extra Terrestrials)? Terra from Latin means land. Extra terra means extra land; therefore, extraterrestrials would mean beings from the extra lands. Could it mean the extra lands exist beyond the supposed south pole, or beyond the north pole?

Try stretching your imagination to go beyond the supposed world map that the controllers provided us with since birth. Not only is the world map distorted, but chunks of land are missing on it too. Reptilians are mind controllers. They exist in the lower astral frequency of the 4th dimension. They can have contact with their minions through rituals on specific holidays through sacrifices, either wars or when there are big gathering events such as sport games, concerts, schools and of course churches.

When these events (movies, concerts, sports etc.) happen, the subconscious mind gets bombarded with subliminal messages in the form of words, sounds and symbols. People unknowingly give their energy to those vampires. Religious people go to church, mosque or any other organized religious institutions thinking they are virtuous without realizing that they worship Satan. All religious buildings are loaded with satanism.

They harvest the souls of the beLIEvers. Reptilians don't know how to love. This is our power over them -"LOVE".

Lower dimensional malevolent entities can show up in your dreams without your invitation, at least on a subconscious level. They can disguise themselves as beautiful women or men and can have an intimate encounter or relationship with you. Either for fun or to download into you, their traits, which are control, destruction, pleasure addictions and any other trait that can keep you from progressing.

Just as you can absorb the trauma or other negative traits from your partner or from another person that you had a one-night stand with, the same things you can take from those entities through your dreams or while you astral travel. You may think they want to help you or that it was just pleasure, but in reality, they manipulate your consciousness, and they lower your vibration.

Everything is energy so it doesn't matter if an intimate encounter happens in your 3d reality or in the 4d lower semi dimensional reality where the malevolent species are. It is just information.

This happens when you are not true to yourself. If you eat unhealthy food, if you consume alcohol, your aura, your electromagnetic field surrounding you, weakens you and you are prone to be penetrated by outside malevolent forces. It's not only about the intimate act.

In your dreams they can just appear to you like your deceased mother, father or any other person that you had a close relationship with, and they can give you advice and you will unknowingly follow the advice. They know very well that if you don't believe they are real then you will panic if they showed their real selves. That's why they disguise themselves as someone you care about.

All of us have reptilian **DNA** . Concrete proof is that before we look like a human in the womb, we look like a reptile first. There are reptilians that are on our team. Some have even converted (reincarnated in regular families) through us to become lightworkers and change their karmic bonds. Reptilian are highly cunning/sharp, very driven intellectuals. They understand how to thrive and navigate the material 3D world better than most people.

A lot of us need space and time to gather ourselves (face our inner shadow/trauma) and our job is to hold space/light. Reptilians can initiate change through the material level. Anyone that inner stands only the physical aspect of life, cannot grasp the concept of a whole lot of worlds that exist in the metaphysical realm. We are just visitors on this Earth, we do not belong in a low frequency world, we belong in a high frequency state of existence.

Unfortunately, there are species in the astral realm using Earth's top elites to create PLANdemics (pandemics) to serve their masters. You must innerstand that to keep low vibrational energies or entities away, affirmations need to be practiced regularly. Malevolent entities cannot stand a person that vibrates with Love. They can only target you if you vibrate in fear, anxiety, lack of abundance, dishonesty etc.

AFFIRMATIONS

- I AM strong, and I do not allow malevolent forces to penetrate my temple.

- I reject indulgent offerings by reptilians or any other malevolent species or any hybrid human beings while awake, or unconscious in my dreams.

- I AM the Light that destroys any form of low vibra tion species that means to harm me.

- Any dark or evil entity is no match for the cosmic Love residing in the center of my heart.

- You will not succeed in influencing me to stray off the path of Light.

- If intimate encounters happen in my dreams, I only allow it to happen with genuine loving human beings and not with malevolent species disguised as beautiful humans by possessing their body in the astral realm.

- I AM encapsulated in Love that no dark forces can destroy.

You have the power of your own mind. Do not leave others to mess with your operating system.

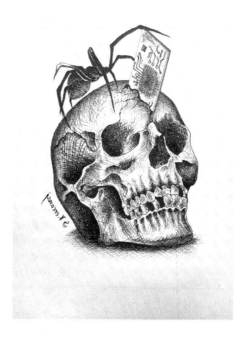

*Resist the chip (metaphorically and literally). Don't give in. By being afraid to die, you might as well call yourself dead already. Nothing is as it seems. Fight the demons inside of you, so you can make room for the Light (**Peace and Freedom**).*

PROTECT YOUR HARD DRIVE

13

SPEAK YOUR MIND

"No one is more hated than he who speaks the truth" - Plato

I will briefly mention one of many situations I have had to deal with throughout my adulthood as an outspoken person. At one of my previous jobs (and everywhere else since I woke up years ago) I always spoke the truth, and I was hated by some people and disliked by some others. I have disliked many people throughout my life, because I didn't know any better. A recent (year 2020) example was not complying about wearing a muzzle (mask). There have had countless situations throughout my life.

One of the workers that disliked me did not talk to me for a week because I was talking with other coworkers about how bad it was to wear the muzzle. One of the managers (I chose not to disclose names) ratted me out to human resources, for private messaging her (outside business hours) about the importance of not wearing masks and I had an exceptionally good relationship with this person. She and many others were complaining about how difficult it was to work with the mask on.

They wanted to do what was right but were immobilized by fear and lack of inner standing. People that lack inner standing and live in fear have bled me for quite some time, to the point that I stopped trying to save others. I innerstood that everyone must save themselves. I do not hold a grudge against anyone. I am happy it happened because I practiced freedom of speech. The situation was more complicated but there is no need to talk about it anymore. I wanted to mention that I never stood down.

I even fought for my coworkers many times and I was seen as the bad guy. Always speak your mind when your sovereignty is threatened. Whenever I mention some personal situations with people, it is not to be condescending. It's for the purpose of this book, and for you the reader to think about similar instances or situations you might have had or will have where your freedom of speech is threatened by other people's compliance. It is true that a negative experience that I have mention, could remind you of an equal or similar negative experience that has happened in your life, but it is needed so you can face the problem.

First you must be aware of it. We consciously let go of certain events but then memories kick in once in a while through someone else's experiences. It reminds us of our own past low vibrational experiences that we had to go through. By being aware of the problem, we take our first step into unrooting the *"cancer"* once and for all. I have had many instances throughout my life where people confided in me (I can be trusted) their personal problems and when I provided them with a personal opinion (solution) they got mad at me.

I will tell you why they got mad. It was because humans want to hear what they want to hear, to satisfy their expectations, or to expect an easy solution. Anything that I suggested, it would mean they would have to put an effort and find a solution, but instead they went into defense mode and gave excuses. They were not open to expanding their thinking and their motivation abilities.

An external solution, (in this case mine) was met with rejection because I shattered their illusion. If you want my opinion, then be prepared that I might not say what you want to hear. Most people live in their own bubble, in their comfortable zone. People feel threatened by someone else's opinion.

Deep down psychologically there is a fear that if they hear someone else's opinion, then they might have to change and believe that new opinion. This is because they are insecure people, and insecurities bring many underlying conditions that create a snowball effect, and it will be exceedingly difficult to get out of that mental self-made prison. When you are true to yourself and when you believe in yourself, you will not feel threatened by external circumstances.

Only the truth will set you free. Your life is your own to live. Do not live it for others. Speak your mind. When you speak the truth you heal yourself, you inspire others to do the same. Your life becomes authentic. Your throat chakra opens by speaking the truth. You vibrate higher. You create a ripple in the universe. Let your spirit/higher self guide you and not your Ego. The closed minded people would rather not think. It is a big responsibility to think.

Many people refuse to work on themselves, so no matter how bad life seems, they say: "**It is what it is**". If they used their brain, they would realize that nothing is at rest. Always changing .

> It never is what it is. It is only what it was not. As the old philosophical/ sacred text saying goes: Cast thy net to the right, which means go right, use the right side of the brain, which is the creative, empathetic, unity side. The left side is for logic, math, statistics, fear and survival. The right side is for nurturing, empathy, and creativity.

Nothing matters more than your personal happiness and your well-being. Just be truthful and you should not mind being questioned. Only the lie does not like to be challenged. Be truthful, be yourself. Other people's opinion shouldn't be your concern. It is not your responsibility to innerstand the version of you other people created in their mind.

> *"The reality you create, is yours and yours only. Nobody can take that away from you. It is your Divine right. You were born with it. Embrace that talent and use it to empower and uplift yourself and humanity." - Saimir K.*

Never apologize for speaking your mind. That's like saying 'sorry' for being real. It is not your responsibility how they filter your words. You can't know how all the people you interact with, will feel at any given time of the day. It is their responsibility to keep they emotions under control.

14

DEATH IS YOUR FRIEND

" It is not death that a man should fear, but he should fear never beginning to live" -Marcus Aurelius

Death is just a change of form. It is like changing your clothes. No need to be afraid. You are changing the outside makeup. Inside, is the real you. Death is not the end, it is walking out of the physical form condensed at a certain vibrational speed, and into the spirit realm/dimension which is your true home. The Earth you are living in, is not your home. You are in school here, to learn. Think of it this way-You die every night. The moment you fall asleep, you are not conscious anymore. As soon as you wake up in the morning you are reborn. A new life begins. The Ego dies. It is the same when you supposedly die at the end of your physical life.

Your ego dies, but the real you will continue living. Your soul is eternal. Do not think of death as a bad thing. A fear of dying derives from an unfulfilled life. It can be unfulfilled from a lack of INNER STANDING.

When you realize that life continues after you die, you will not fear death anymore. Death can be your friend. Death does not exist. I know, it is terrifying (it was for me once but not anymore). The thought of leaving this world forever and not existing, is scary and leaves you with no purpose.

You will just change form. It's your lower mind EGO that is scared of death. Ego exists only through fear. I have realized that I AM eternal. I am not scared to die. You will realize it too. Does that mean that I do not care if I die anytime? No, but not because I am scared and don't want to die. It is because I love my life and want to enjoy this beautiful world with everything in it. So when it is time to die then an eternal realization becomes present/known to you.

My point of view is based on me loving myself. When you love yourself, you love everyone. Through many different exercises and new patterns of thoughts and actions, I got rid of the fear of dying. You can too. Dying in your sleep is the best way to DIE. No one would like to suffer before dying. Many parents are scared to die before their children, and that is understandable.

By living in fear, negative energy gets latched onto your children and they also live in fear. If you teach them love, and that we are here temporarily and that life continues, then you gave them a priceless lesson. You can have all the money in the world, but if your children are unhappy and empty inside, then money and materialism are useless.

The word death sounds terrifying to most people. I bought a book in 2019 written by SENECA, the wise advisor of NERO, called "How to DIE". Nine out of 10 people I knew, thought I was crazy for buying it. Their facial expression was as if they were already thinking about their own death. It is how powerful a word can be.

This derives from your memories of the times you read or heard the word death. From every time you heard about someone dying, every time you watched a movie or a show talking about death.

You were bombarded consciously and also subconsciously. Consciously is when you read about it in the moment, but subconsciously it gets recorded and will surface every time you are presented to any situation where the word "death" is mentioned, written or the action of dying or killing is seen.

It creates an illusion in your head. When you get scared of something, you are not supposed to ignore it but you are to study it and embrace it. Fear is in your head. I am not talking about studying the teeth of a tiger that's about to eat you. That is dangerous.

Danger is real. Fear is all created in your head as a result of your memories. If you live in the moment, there is no such thing as fear. Unless you consciously embrace death (darkness) and become friends, you will never appreciate life (Light). This is an absolute fact. Death and Life are two sides of the same coin. There is nothing to fear. Besides, after you die you do not feel any pain, so why worry? Dying is like going to sleep. It is the same as fearing to fall asleep. You are not afraid to go to sleep because you know you will wake up again the next day.

The only difference with the real (supposed) death is that you either wake up in the form of incarnation, which you will start from scratch as a baby and will not remember anything from your previous life, or you will continue living in higher dimension/realm depending on how high you ascended from in this incarnation/life. You will carry inside of you other people from many generations who came before you.

When you die, you get married for eternity. You must never take your own life. You (your soul/higher self) signed a contract before entering this world. You, like everyone else, have a mission. Most people die between 25-30 and get buried at 75 plus. You die the moment you stop living your life and just to exist. Have you noticed that children always ask questions? It's because they are not tainted by adulthood yet.

When you stop asking questions, you die. What is the point of existing physically when life passes you by without enjoying it? By remaining a child, you will never die mentally and emotionally. You die physically but remain an immortal spirit.

As Marcus Aurelius said:

> *"I will throw you into prison. Correction - It is my body you will throw there "*

Marcus Aurelius means that he is free, his mind and soul are free, his body is just a vehicle with an expiry date like our own. You can imprison my body but not my mind and soul. Be free like animals. Not like the ones you see in a cage.

No matter how unsupportive/unbearable life may seem, know that it is a lesson to go higher on the spiritual ladder and progress. When you are at the bottom, you can only go up. Every human being is strong, but not all can unleash their inner strength. Some choose a suicidal path and that is the wrong way to exit in this realm. Taking your own life is never the answer. You cannot cheat your way out of this life. You must honour the contract (*spiritual contract*) that you came here to fulfill. I have a question for you:

Q - Are you alive?
A - Yes, of course.

Therefore, your work/mission is not complete in this realm we call Earth. Befriend your death (metaphorically, when the ego dies) so that you can be reborn and continue your mission without distractions. It is up to you what your mission/purpose is in this incarnation. My mission is to help humanity by uplifting/empowering people through my books, social media or anytime I meet someone in real life (whatever real life means).

That's on you to figure out your calling. You will not be able to figure that out if you are constantly being distracted by people or things (materialistic things such as: Technological gadgets, cars, clothes etc. Anything external that you distract yourself with, will stay here. You cannot take it with you in the next life/form/reality.

Your flesh body is your temporary shell.
The inner universe is eternal.

15

ANIMALS ARE OUR COMPANIONS

Anything in nature is intelligent. The animals are super intelligent in their own way. Birds, insects create beautiful geometric shaped nests. If you observe them without analyzing anything about them, you will realize that we are not much different from them. I had bunnies years ago. I remember, one of them got pregnant and I saw her looking around for hay to build a warm nest for her baby bunnies. She was going to have the babies the next day. In the evening, I saw her pull off chunks of her own fur and I was like "*Is she crazy*"?

I was a city boy, I had no experience with animals. I figured out the fur she was pulling off was for the nest she was trying to build. I was amazed at that simple fact. When the babies were born, I tried to pick up one of the little cuties and guess what, the mother did not take care of the one I picked up, so the baby died. Just so you know, use a paper towel or a cloth to pick up a baby bunny that does not have any fur yet.

Your human scent goes onto the baby's skin and the mother will smell it and abandon the baby. Animals are highly intelligent. We humans don't think animals are intelligent. We think because the animals don't speak like us, that makes them dumb. I have never seen an animal line up to get a flu shot (or any other type of vaccination), have you? An animal would not eat poisoned food. Humans do.

Animals know the order of things, meaning they know what they have to do, to live in accordance with nature. They know what awaits them on the other side of the physical life. An antelope would not go close up to a tiger to say "hello"! They can sense the energy of other animals. We can too, but our analytical mind and our desires make us ignore what really matters, which is living in harmony with each other. Animals do not work nonstop to put fake illusioned currency in the bank for an unknown meaningless date. They just want to eat and survive and live-in harmony.

We humans were once like that, but then something happened, and we distanced ourselves from nature. If you observe animals closely, you can learn a lot from them, especially love and compassion. It is your duty to protect animals from cruelty. You must be concerned with your own morals. Eating them is cannibalism, even if you cook it. Think with your mind, starve your belly, do not let your belly and/or taste buds be your mind's boss.

Discipline yourself so that anything that gets
thrown at you, doesn't have a chance at
jeopardizing the flow of your existence.

No animal is more worthy than another. Deep down, we all love animals. Why do we call them "pets" and others dinner? Is it because we have been conditioned to think so? That's what it is. Love all animals. Respect them all. Every animal has a purpose, and that purpose is to not be consumed by humans.

Not consuming rotten flesh is one of the keys to ascend to a higher frequency. You can't expect a peaceful loving society by devouring another species. You are not more important than them.

Respect all life forms so that you will be equally respected back.

"Animals are the doorway to spiritual progress on a physical level.
Meditation is the doorway on a metaphysical level. Both of these are
interconnected. Animals may be physical beings to you, but they are
metaphysical (spirits) in their true state of existence, just as you are"
- Saimir K.

You'll know when your frequency/vibration is rising, when:

Animals feel safe in your presence.
You'll know because they will approach you frequently. They are sent to you for a reason. Do not deny them. Have you noticed that as time goes on, more and more people have pets? It means that the humanity's frequency is rising. The experiment is proving to be a success. The experiment of raising the consciousness of the Earth's inhabitants in such a short period of time. A few decades is very short time compared to many thousands of years that humanity was in a coma/asleep state.

Some other signs that your vibration is high or rising are:

People stare at you in public.

The one staring at you could be either a high or a low vibratio person. Those that are vibrate higher, feel magnetized toward you, they feel like you are their family because you vibrate in the same/similar frequency. Those that are low energetically/vibrationally stare at you because they either want to know/have what you do, or they are jealous of you and they might want to destroy you because your strength shines very bright on their weakness.

If you are self-confident, strong minded and emotionally strong, then they won't be able to face your light. They will weed themselves out of your life. You might know people that are negative/mean, but at the same time they have pets. Do you know what that is? That is because they have to learn empathy through sharing their life with their pets. Their pet chose them and not the other way around.

Random strangers come to you and talk, and confide their stories with you.

On a spiritual level the souls of two people communicate instantly without words. On a physical level a person need words to communicate, and they cannot infringe free will. When someone randomly comes to you and talks about personal stuff, they are already aligned with you spiritually.

You just don't know it on a conscious level. Do not dismiss situations like this. The person that randomly talks to you could be one of your guides who are initiated to help you on a spiritual level. Your guide will give you messages in a million ways. Those messages could be Through your family member, co-worker, a stranger, an animal of even the wind. How can the wind give you a message you might ask? Let's say you are in a dilemma about something, and you have to decide whether to do something or not.

> _If you lean toward doing/saying something bad that could implicate your life in a negative way, the spiritual guide (which is an etheric/ energetic being) will manipulate the air around you and create a little breeze. You will feel that breeze and your attention will/might be to turn away from the bad choice, and you might/will be inclined to take the positive choice._

You might still decide a negative outcome if you are dominated by negative thoughts/state of mind. The guides only give you suggestions, and in the end it is you that decides what to do. No matter what you decide, you will keep repeating the same lessons until you make the positive choice, to help align with the betterment of your life and humanity's as a whole. Ultimately, we all strive to get to the same destination.

Just be careful that you don't miss the journey while focusing on the destination. The journey (enjoying every moment) is more rewarding than the destination. How? If you miss many enjoyable things in life, in the after life when you look at all the things that you did or did not do, you might decide to reincarnate again in this realm. It is better to engage with love in anything that you do and not have any regrets.

You can feel the energy of a room shift when you walk in.

Depending on how vibrationally high you are, you can easily feel the energy shift. During the modern day lifestyle, our buildings/rooms are like boxes/cubes, the energy is stagnant, especially in the corners of the rooms. If the buildings were round/domes, (as in the ancient times, in certain periods) the energy would freely flow without any disruption. When you walk in a room, especially when there is very stagnant energy, you will feel the sudden shift of energy. See the stagnant energy as DARK, and the high vibrational free flowing energy as LIGHT.

> Cats are spiritual animals. If you have a cat, the stagnant energy (which might also be an etheric low vibration entity), will try and escape because it can't stand high frequency energy beings such as a cat.

You irritate toxic people just by being your TRUE and AUTHENTIC self.

As previously stated about the stagnant energy being DARK and the free flowing one being LIGHT, it will apply the same way between two people. We all are electromagnetic beings. We affect each other in positive or negative ways. If you irritate someone by being yourself, you are doing what you are supposed to be doing - **Shining your light.**

If you irritate someone on purpose, then it's not shining your light. Unless you are planting the seed of healing. If someone gets irritated by you then they must work on themselves and achieve emotional balance. Always remember that everyone has the right to exercise their free will. No matter how right you may think you are, if they do not want to progress, it is their choice. Your job is only to warn them by shining the light on their path.

Let them decide if they want to initiate their trip toward the destination. Let's say that you are the one that is toxic. If you are irritating someone then they are not as healed as they think they may be. It is their job to not give attention to your words or actions, unless you do something that affects them in a bad way. They still must realize that we all are actors in this movie called life. They can choose to play out the script/contract that they have with you or break/nullify it by moving on and sailing toward new horizons.

If a friend is not compatible with you after a few years, then you don't have to be friends with them for the rest of your life. Make new friends. New friends will bring new knowledge/wisdom to you. The same applies for when two partners don't get along. You don't have to stay with them for a long time or for the rest of your life. Expand your horizons and don't be caught in memories of past relationships.

Many people are happy to live with a dog or a cat and that's perfectly fine. An animal can teach empathy much faster than a human. An animal doesn't care how you look like, how much money you have etc. Animals love humans unconditionally. After all, that's one of the reasons they exist. Imagine a world without animals, birds or bugs. Take all the time you need. There would not be life without them. They are the blocks of the ecosystem.

Look at your pet (or any animal) in the eyes.
WHAT DO YOU SEE?

16

WHY DO WE AGE ?

W hy do we age ? I will try to explain as best as I can. There is not a fast and easy solution without inner standing. Even if you are a very open-minded person, there is still a process that must take place. The moment you were born, do you feel you started to die or started to live? Both are right, depending on the mindset and the perspective of the individual based on the memories of the past or the vision of the future. Both the past and the future are illusions which dictate the present being real. Even the present being real is debatable.

Personally, since I woke up to this illusion called "conditioned life", I have started to live. When you die physically, you will continue living but just in a different form, either as an animal, another physical/semi-physical being or a spirit. Age is an illusion created by the "ego" mind. Ego is one of the 7 levels of minds. You live in constant search of an illusion, or a reality that you think is real. What you are searching for is not real. Anything you really need, will come to you when you align with the Creator/Universe [check the beginning of the Chapter WHAT OR WHO IS GOD for one of the interpretations people have of the Creator]. You think it is real because of the parameters you have encapsulated yourself with. Those parameters are:

1-Negatives that deceive you into thinking they are positives.

2-Positives, deceiving you into thinking they are positives.

They are both immobilizers.

NEGATIVES DELUDING YOU

Working for retirement / Fear of dying / Paradise-Hell / Satisfying other people's expectations / Competing for more / People pleaser

Working for retirement locks you in a hamster wheel of a mental and physical state. You are overwhelmed with an everyday busy anxious life and achieving something unknown in the future. The future does not exist. Focusing on retirement, makes you forget to live your life. This happens when you reach a certain age and you start feeling old.

It is absurd to put parents in retirement homes. This comes as a result of the lifestyle you live, the person you are married to, and people that you associate yourself with. In a couple, both of you affect each other .

One of the two doesn't have feelings for the parents of their spouse and so they don't want to live with them. I am talking about when parents are at a certain point when they can't take care of themselves. This also influences you into getting older because by not having them home and taking care of them, you are telling your cells to get older as opposed to if you were vibrating in love frequency.

You think of your parents as being old and dying soon or eventually . You are reminded of this thing constantly by your thoughts or other people that influence you on a daily basis. Your internal biology gets the orders from the perception you have of the outside world. I am talking about the cells in this case.

Fear of dying comes from lack of inner standing the importance of living in the present, the "NOW" and lack of inner standing that life is just a dream. Death is an illusion. It is ingrained into your brain since birth. Fear of dying puts you in debt. How so? "Unfulfilled life". You want a car, a house, gadgets and all sorts of things to make you happy within this lifetime frame without truly realizing that happiness is where you are, without the need to go anywhere.

Even if you get those things, you will eventually want a better car, a better house, better clothes etc. Totally conditioned by society. The more you have the more you want. There is no end to the desire to have more. Money will not bring you happiness. As Bob Marley said:

> *"Money is just numbers and numbers never end. If it requires money to reach happiness, the search for happiness will never end".*

Paradise/hell-Terms enforced upon you by organized religion. Regardless of if you are a religious person or not. The fact that you hear these terms throughout your life by all kinds of people, causes you to believe that illusion subconsciously. Hearing something many times gets recorded in your subconscious, regardless if you believe it or not. Paradise and hell are not places, but states of mind. They are different levels of consciousness.

Paradise consciousness or your mindset level operates in LOVE. Hell operates in fear. These states of consciousness cannot live together. Either you vibrate in love or you vibrate in fear. It is an epidemic in our society in relationships, be it husband and wife or coworkers or friends that when one of the two vibrates in an opposite energetic field to the other, we all have divorces and problems between those groups of people.

Both groups of people that vibrate in opposite states of mind, are both right in their level of innerstanding.

One of them lives in hell, the other is trying to live in paradise. I said try because they don't want to lose the other person. It is from the fear of being alone. Even if you are a good person, by not being yourself and not wanting to hurt the other person, you still hurt that person in the long run. You are giving a hand to the other person in postponing their own beginning of rebirth. Organized religion made sure throughout centuries to condition people to look for answers externally.

They conditioned people to think and belIEve that God is a person in the sky, and the devil is the red guy with a pitchfork. Even if you are a religious person and don't believe that the devil is the red guy, it doesn't matter. Your subconscious has already been bombarded since birth, unless you are on the road of looking within, then you are good.

People pleaser-Satisfying other people's expectations. Wanting to please others, is destroying yourself. Unless your intention is genuine and the others receiving your blessings are genuine. By wanting to please others to be seen as an important person, you lack confidence in yourself. You don't know your value. If you don't know your worth, don't expect others to know your worth. Others will value you less. Every time you do something to please someone to get something in return, you lose a piece of yourself.

Competing for more
Trying to compete with someone that has more than you, is a total delusion, a fear of not being left behind. By trying to reach someone else's status or achievement level, you forget and neglect those people around you that genuinely care about you. You are not appreciating the moment. Every breath you take is all you have. That's living your life.

Competing for a status/position at work or in any relationship. That will entice you to be dishonest, greedy or jealous and may end up hurting people (directly, indirectly and physically or mentally) just to get what you want. Trust me, I've been there and some of you have already been through this as well. Everyone would behave this way if they were forced into a corner against their will. If you put an animal into a corner it will bite you. Nobody likes to be forced.

That's a lesson to be learned. If you do nothing about it, as many are not, you will hurt people you hang out with. Because of your drama and your lower vibrational frequency. Your negativity will spread throughout all the environments you interact with. We are all connected, and everything is connected.

You may wonder what all this has to do with aging. It definitely has to do with aging. Keep reading and it will make sense, although you might not like the truth. If it doesn't make sense to some of you, you will have to shed the weight that is buried deep inside your mind. We will talk about that "weight" as we go.

POSITIVES DELUDING YOU

Birthday / Holiday / Getting a raise at work/ Party / Showing off achievements / Retirement waiting / Drinking / Marriage / Wanting to have children.

Celebrating the Birthday of a child is an amazing experience. I have children myself. It's a wonderful thing for parents and the people that know those parents, assuming those people are genuinely happy for that new life, or an old life in a repeated cycle/reincarnation. That's fine saying *Happy Birthday* for the first couple of years to the child. The moment the child inner stands that after the number 2, comes number 3 then 4 and so on, then his/her subconscious gets recorded/conditioned for death. You may be asking- What is this guy talking about? - Keep reading.

Numbers don't end, but when we use them within the context of a human physical life then they end at 70, 80 or whatever age we die (remember, the real YOU, the higher mind never dies). Your ego or lower mind takes hold of your emotions and thoughts.- Emotions are preceded by thoughts, remember? Every year you say *"Happy birthday"* to your children or to other people. When it's your birthday, you hear the same words by others wishing you a happy birthday. Besides genuine people, there are also fake people wishing you a happy life, but they don't really mean it.

Receiving birthday wishes or gifts from people that don't care about you will generate negative feelings around you and in your subconscious. By reading this section, the words "happy birthday" are also increasingly adding to your subconscious. Although the word happy is a positive word, as far as age goes, in your subconscious it turns into a negative immobilizing obstacle.

The number of your age, the word "old" and the beLIEf that you age, influence your trillions of cells that make your physical body. You have been bombarded countless times. Your subconscious dictates your conscious life. Before you even begin celebrating your birthday, you think about it many times. You think about your appareance, gifts, party and so on. How many times do you hear it from coworkers, family members and so on? Also, in social media I'm disgusted by the sheer amount from fakeness of people that pretend to be happy for you.

Just for that one day. Now multiply it with all the years you have lived up to now. You will get yourself in the midst of an illusion my dear friend. Wishing Happy Birthday only tells you that you are getting closer to death. This applies when you are scared of dying. In my case, you can tell me "happy birthday" all day long. It will not affect me. Your ego mind thinks only temporarily, but the time will come when you will pay for it if you don't stop certain meaningless habits. Needing to celebrate all the time means that you are not capable of living in solitude, it means you need the gratifications to cope with the emptiness.

If we lived in a world where people truly cared about each other unconditionally, then it would be awesome to celebrate. Alas, we live in a world of illusion where fakeness, selfishness and materialism have choked the life out of us. Celebrating certain meaningless illusions only adds salt to the wound. It's like getting full with an empty spoon. I don't celebrate my birthday as there is nothing to celebrate. I celebrate every day when I open my eyes. I am born every day from the moment I wake up in this dream called life. If you celebrate your birthday, you only celebrate the past. What does that mean for the present? You are giving hope to yourself based on a past event.

Not only are you not in the present, you are also setting yourself up for future disappointment. I can't make you innerstand this, you are the one that has to innerstand it. You will innerstand if you lay off the weight that has been put on you by society from a lifetime of conditioning.

The birthday that everyone celebrates is actually a death celebration. The birthday date is the date that your STRAWMAN was created. You are a living soul, not a 2D fictional entity (strawman) on paper. You were born half alive. They cut the umbilical cord, took the placenta and vandalized you and everyone. That placenta was used as a deposit/ on hold for when you reclaim it back. So, all life you pay taxes, fines, speeding/parking tickets that are entirely optional. All those things are not for you but for the fake fictional strawman. You were deceived big time. It is time that you become free by releasing the STRAWMAN. You are a living soul, not a dead legal fictional character. By the way, the cake that people eat on birthdays, is actually symbolizing the placenta. Placenta in Greek means cake. So, birthday is actually a death day. The real birthday is when the fertilization happened.

To learn more on the STRAWMAN subject, read the book: **YOU ARE NOT A STRAWMAN YOU ARE THE ZYGOTE** *by Saimir X. Kercanaj*

Depending on your age and life experience, you might have to go deep into the darkness of your soul, (unless you have already been there) it will be a lot easier when you regularly practice affirmations, meditation and being mindful daily. Every time someone asks "how old are you?", the number of your age and the word "old" automatically puts you into a fear of death mode-Subconsciously. You don't realize it, but it definitely does.

Never underestimate the power of your subconscious mind, one of the 7 levels of minds. Subconsciousness will be explored in a different chapter and if you innerstand how powerful your subconscious is, then you will innerstand this chapter with ease. I purposely put the subconscious chapter for later on.

So, instead of asking "how old are you?", how about we ask - "how YOUNG are you?"

If it is ok (it's not) to ask "how old are you?" to an older person, it shouldn't be okay to ask the same question to a younger person or children.

The asking of "how old are you?" was purposefully enforced to be said that way with the purpose to control. If we lived a long time, then we would figure out THEIR (powers that be) game. The veil is lifting though.

By listening to the word "young" repeatedly, you program your subconscious for life, not for death. Test it with family members or coworkers. They may look like you are weird or crazy, but you and I already know now who the crazy ones are.

Programming subconsciousness with these sayings applies only for the language that you are speaking/thinking. If a German asked you how old you are a thousand times a day, it wouldn't affect you if you didn't innerstand the language. If the German (or any other nationality) wishes you harm constantly it would damage your AURA, the outside energetic field you are surrounded with, regardless if you understand their language or not. The Universe does not speak English or French or any other language.

The more damaged your energetic field is, the more of a magnet you are for evil external forces to latch onto you. Evil forces are greed, lust, selfishness, guilt, resentment, unforgiveness etc.

If you hang around people that vibrate in low vibration and have those negative traits, you will be greatly affected and infected. The purpose of this section is not about ignoring the fact that you will be getting older. It's about you innerstanding "the why ", and when you innerstand the why and apply the affirmations daily, then you will innerstand how powerful you are by default without the need of fake light from external sources.

The light is within you. Any external light will only make you dim. After you manage to be in charge of your life, then nobody's word can harm you. The tongue (words) does not have any bones, but it can break bones. Meaning by using words , you can hurt someone without any physical weapon.

Someone can hurt you if you fall prey to their bad words (negative energy) or any other external energies. What I'm writing has to do with the level of inner standing based on the experience I have now. I have gray hair already. Where I used to work, people joked and made fun of me and said "you are getting older". I'm like, "Nope I'm getting younger toward my next incarnation", I'm full of energy. Some of them said, "Where do you find this energy man?" I said *"It's with me all the time, everyone is full of energy. You just need to unlock that energy. It's the perception of the outside world that dictates your inner peace/biology"*.

If you have a healed body, mind and soul, outside things/people will not affect you. Unless it's a situation like the Plandemic (*I'm writing this in the middle of the fake virus, or real virus if you believe it to be so*). You might say that a lot of people that wear a mask don't believe in the CONrona, those people were forced one way or another). Even if that is true, by obeying the tyrannical system it's the same as believing in the virus, which the virus in this case is *"the system"*.

A healed person is a fortress. This is not to put down other people. Firstly, you are responsible for yourself, then you are responsible for your children if they haven't reached the age of reason yet. If you have not healed yourself, not only can you not heal another person, but you will also damage that person. Some of you may strongly disagree, and that's good. If you agree with everything I write, then you can't learn anything new, or your way of thinking won't get challenged. We can't grow if we agree on everything.

As long as you don't dismiss anything you don't innerstand. By now you have noticed that I only use the word "innerstand", instead of UNDERstand. Understanding means that you stand under authority. When the police pulls you over and asks "Do you understand?", they are actually asking,

Do you stand under authority?

Unknowing you say *"YES"*. The moment you say yes, you are binding into a verbal CONtract with the state. When you use the word INNERstand, it means that you understand from within, you are your own authority, and you don't stand under external ones.

Beside the above section where I used the word understand a couple times, if you find it written anywhere else, points for you. If I had read this book years ago, I would think this author (me) was crazy. Now at this point in my life I'm being called crazy many times from people that are at a level of understanding (I was under others' authority) that I myself was years ago. That's a compliment. I innerstand them but they don't innerstand me.

My friend *** ******* inner stands me the most. He makes fun of my accent and I forgive him. I got free coffee from him many times because I forgot to bring my own coffee, or maybe I forgot on purpose. - I'm laughing right now, without an accent though. Well, I'm not sure you can hear an accent when someone's laughing, can *you? The people that innerstand you the most are those that can empower you, providing their intention toward you is genuine.*

Happy life

Many say that they want to be happy. Happiness won't arrive if you wait for it. Happiness is a state of mind. The waiting creates anxiety. The waiting will be awfully long, and happiness will never come if you keep waiting to have something you already have but had no idea it was present with you this whole time.

Remember? Perception of how you see the outside world will dictate the world inside of you. The world inside you is the way you think. Your mind (subconscious) controls the whole world inside of you, your thinking, organ function, cells etc. You think consciously but if you are not healed, your subconscious will be the captain of the ship (you). You might not admit it but there is another person inside of you that controls you.

I AM eight years young. Eight years ago, I was born. You are born the moment you are hatched out of ignorance. How young are you? All these factors are conditioning your cells for living or self-destructing. In the words of Mahatma Gandhi:

Your beliefs become your thoughts-

Your thoughts become your words

Your words become your actions

Your actions become your habits

Your habits become your values

Your values become your destiny

So, why do we age?

We age because the mind controls the cells and the genes. We collectively believe in aging. The environment controls the fate of your cells. Your genes do not control your inner biology. The outside environment influences the behavior of cells without changing the genetic code. It is a lie that diseases are hereditary. People don't innerstand the power of the subconscious mind and its ability to record any belief that you have.

So, if you believe that you will get cancer because your mother or father did, then chances of you getting it are much higher. You will innerstand better when you read the subconscious chapter. Choose your destiny, Life or Death. Life asked death, *"Why do people love me and hate you?"* Death replied, *"Because you are a beautiful lie, and I AM a beautiful truth."*

Do we talk about trees getting older? No. We say that they are growing. Shouldn't we use the same term for when we talk about HUMANS? We are not getting older, we are growing, we are expanding. Think like this and you will watch your life become a certain paradise.

AFFIRMATIONS:

- I AM young and forever will be.
- Death is the beginning of life.
- I must die (metaphorically) so I can be reborn.
- Every day I become younger.
- My birthday is every sunrise (Footnote #4) when I open my eyes.
- Everyone I know is just as young as me.
- Death (physical) is the beginning of another life.

17

FEAR - THE INVISIBLE MONSTER

F ear exists as a result of memories of the past and anxiety for the future. The past is already gone, the future hasn't happened yet, and yet the consequences of both past and future lurk within your everyday life activities. There is never a reason to fear anything. Don't mistake fear with "worry", although worries are related to fear. As long as worries are temporary, then they can become the last step before the beginning of empowering choices that lead to the liberation of your illusioned, imprisoned self.

You are a sovereign being and must take ownership of your mental, emotional and physical health. Do not fall or get distracted by the fear controlled distorted reality that convinces you that you are powerless. You are anything but powerless. In general people say *"this or that"* sucks when it's raining or when i's cold or when something is not to their liking.

Nothing "sucks". If we observe and appreciate things for what they are and instead of what we want them to be then we will see that nature is beautiful. What happens in nature cannot change based on your liking. You must change the thoughts and reactions you have of those. You will realize that all the sadness, drama and fear were only in your head in the form of thoughts. Fear kills you slowly. When you are frightened regularly, you become dumber. Teachers see it all the time among students who don't test well. It doesn't mean that the students are dumb. It just means that anxiety and fear of scoring low causes the students to not do well. Exam stress usually paralyses many students who mark the wrong answers because of panic. They can't access cerebrally stored information they have carefully acquired all semester.

The Hypothalamic Pituitary Adrenal HPA (Footnote #5) system is a brilliant mechanism for handling acute stress. This protection system was not designed to be continuously activated. In today's world, most of the stress we are experiencing is not in the form of concrete threats that we can easily identify, respond to and move on from. We are constantly besieged by multitudes of unresolvable worries about our personal lives, our jobs and our global community being destroyed by wars, (visible or non-visible (*mental*).

Such worries do not threaten our immediate survival, but they nevertheless can activate the HPA axis, resulting in chronically elevated stress hormones. The stress becomes chronic and results in a sustained release of the adrenal glucocorticoid hormone cortisol.

Overstimulation of this hormone is linked to significant damage and long-lasting functional changes in the brain. By being in constant worry and fear, you are being kept in constant stress. Stress and the functions of stress hormones is to take energy from the body and get it all to run and fight (fight or flight). The stress hormone will shut off the functions of things that will not be needed in fight or flight (survival mode).

One of the most important uses of energy in the body is the immune system. Stress hormones shut off the immune system. The significance is that every one of us is infected with almost all of the disease germs that humans have such as viruses, bacteria, parasites. You might ask: If you are infected, then why are you not sick? If your immune system works properly, then it will suppress these parasites and germs.

The moment you start to shut off the immune system, the organisms begin to start growing again, so the idea that you can catch a disease is not technically true. You already have the disease, and the medical people call these germs *opportunistic organisms.* If you are under stress and shut off the immune system, then you give these organisms the opportunity to then make the disease.

When you are constantly worried and in fear, the blood will go from the front of the head where consciousness is, to the back where reflexes are. By being in survival mode the blood concentrates in your legs, arms and back of the head for survival.

This is fine if the danger is temporary, but let's say you have to escape from a tiger or a lion (assuming you can), being in survival mode is normal. When that kind of danger is gone then everything returns to normal.

BUT:

When you are in constant stress and fear every day, then you become less intelligent.

This is a fact. Not only were studies done, but even common sense should tell you that if there was not enough blood/oxygen in your brain, especially in the front where consciousness is, then you would be dumbed down.

Why neglect your potential?

You have two choices:

EITHER	OR
F. Face	**F.** Forget
E. Everything	**E.** Everything
A. And	**A.** And
R. Rise	**R.** Run

Run all you want: the shadow is faster than you. Better to face your fears so you can accelerate the process of overcoming the contraption that you have created out of a delusion called "*FEAR*"

AFFIRMATIONS

- I AM brave and have no fear.
- No one can put me in a fear-based state.
- I vibrate in love and fear is nonexistent in this state.
- Stress is a thing of the past; I AM focusing on new horizons.
- My frequency is rising beyond that of the low vibra tonal fear frequency.
- I will not let the fear of the unknown future immo bilize me.

The monster cannot exist without your permission.

LET IT GO

Fear is just a visitor
and not a resident in your mind.

Fear is an invisible enemy created by your lower mind EGO. When an animal or a human (not all) wants to attack you, they look into your eyes first to see if you are controlled by the invisible enemy. Nothing, absolutely nothing is worth being afraid of.

18

DARKNESS IS THE SEED OF LIFE

"Darkness cannot drive out darkness, only Light can do that. Hate cannot drive out hate, only Love can do that"

-Martin Luther King, Jr

What is darkness? Why are we scared of it? Is it the end or the beginning of life? Metaphorically and literally, darkness can breed both death and life. Metaphorically speaking, your old, disempowered, self-destroyed way of life can die and a new self-uplifting, self-empowered being can be reborn. While literally dying physically can also bring salvation or destruction. Destruction of your physical self can be death if you have accumulated bad karma throughout this or other past lives. It can bring a metaphorical death to those loved ones that have played a great role in helping you, but it can also bring death to you which you must carry in the afterlife in the form of having to reincarnate again and learn the unfinished lessons of the previous lifetime.

If you have accumulated good karma, then a physical death can breed life by being reborn again. You could be reborn in a different but higher frequency dimension or in this one if you willingly choose to reincarnate again on a three-dimensional dense plane to help humanity. Just like Jesus, St. Germaine, Buddha, Krishna, Isis, Socrates and many other ascended masters did. Whether these spiritual masters actually were physical beings or not, it doesn't matter.

> *We must learn to not associate darkness with evil. Yes, when evil things happen, we tend to associate it with darkness. Throughout human history, evil things have always happened. A narrative that promoted evil directly or indirectly to keep us scared and afraid of dying at all times. As a result we were kept at a low vibrational frequency out of ignorance.*

People would associate anything bad with darkness without realizing that most of the suffering and struggling in our life is our doing. When we don't innerstand certain bad things, we either ignore or label them as evil. Unless we recognize things for what they are, suffering will always participate in our life.

If you close your eyes any time, or while you are meditating, you will see darkness. The Night sky is dark. When you plant a seed in the ground, the seed grows in darkness within the soil. A new life that a mother carries in her womb grows in darkness. When we do shadow work (inner reflection), we face our darkness before seeing the light. When we die, we close our eyes, and it is a darkness from our physical viewpoint. Our universe was created out of the void which is darkness. Darkness breeds creation of all life forms. What is there to be afraid of ?

Our purpose is to kindle a light in the vastness of darkness. There cannot be light without darkness and vice versa. Do not think of death as darkness. Evil is darkness, or a better way of describing evil would be "distorted light".

Here is a little story about darkness being the catalyst for the light, instead of being scared and paralyzed from it.

In a mother's womb were two babies. One asked the other:

"Do you believe in life after delivery?"

The other replied, "Of course, there has to be something after delivery. Maybe we are here to prepare ourselves for what will be later."

"Nonsense", said the first baby. *"There is no life after delivery. What kind of life would that be?"*

The second one said: "I don't know, but there will be more light than here. Maybe we will walk with our legs and eat with our mouths. Maybe we will have other senses that we can't innerstand now."

The first one replied: *"That is absurd. Walking is impossible. Eating with our mouths? Ridiculous! The umbilical cord supplies nutrition and everything we need but the umbilical cord is short. Life after delivery is to be logically excluded."*

The second insisted, "Well, I think there is something and maybe it is different than it is here. Maybe we won't need this physical cord anymore."

The first baby replied: *"Nonsense. And moreover, if there is life, then why has no one ever come back from there? Delivery is the end of life, and in the after-delivery, there is nothing but darkness, silence and oblivion. It takes us nowhere."*

"Well, I don't know," **said the second,** "but certainly we will meet our Mother and she will take care of us"

The first replied, *"Mother? You actually believe in a Mother? That's laughable. If a Mother exists, then where is she now?"*

The second said, "She is all around us. We are surrounded by Her. We are Her. It is in Her that we live. Without Her, this world would not and could not exist."

The first one said: *"Well, I don't see Her, so it is only logical that She doesn't exist."*

To which the second replied, "Sometimes, when you are in silence and focus and listen, you can perceive Her presence, and you can hear Her loving voice, calling down from above and from within."

What do we learn from this beautiful story? The Mother/Creator is all around us, in us and everywhere. It is a matter of listening in silence, that's when the Creator becomes visible in our perception, as far as listening and feeling Creator from the depth of our hearts. As far as seeing the Creator with our own eyes, all we have to do is to look at the nature, at us, at everything.

Everything is a result of the Divine Creator. You might ask: Since there are people out there that are not as loving as some others, why then would the Creator create those people? It is fair that we all exercise free will, even when the "not so loving people" have the same divine rights as you do.

The difference is that they are still in the womb (metaphorically), which means they are still in darkness and have not realized that there is light outside of the womb. The darkness is part of the creation, it is needed to catapult you into the Light. At one point you too, were in the womb.

It may seem like we are in dark times, which literally we are. We are in the WOMB between the old and the new. Just like when the baby is in the womb or in the wom(b)an. Collectively we are in the birthing canal. The energies are working for us and not against us. Just as a woman has contractions before giving birth to a new life, so does Gaia (Earth) has its own contractions in the form of earthquakes, volcanos, fires and so on. Earth is going through the birthing process and so are we.

WE

ARE

TRANSMUTING

DARKNESS

INTO

LIGHT.

Balance feminine and masculine energies.

A strong woman knows she has strength for the journey, but a woman of strength knows it is the journey that will help her become strong. Be the Goddess who honors your body as the sacred temple of the Spirit of Life, with each inhale serving as a prayer of gratitude. (This applies to *both* genders)

19

WOMEN/MEN, GODS & GODDESSES OF THE UNIVERSE

" The feminine is more powerful than the masculine, the soft is more powerful than the hard, the water is more powerful than the rock" - OSHO

Woman is the Goddess that created everything. If God was a person, it had to be a woman. Men have always destroyed. That's because the controllers have suppressed the women's power, meaning the feminine aspect of the male's brain but also they have suppressed the feminine aspect in many women to the point that many of them have become masculine. If men developed a healthy feminine aspect of the mind then there wouldn't be any wars. The feminine aspect is about nurturing and compassion. There is a great need for the feminine and the masculine to be balanced again. Everything was created, virtually "out of thin air".

The child is created in the womb. Although female/male is a duality aspect, both feminine and masculine energies are needed. I wanted to mention this for the macho men that might have misunderstood the importance of the feminine aspect of life. Men and women both have feminine and masculine aspects to them. To have peace in this world, women must rise higher, and men must work on their ego. This is an interesting subject.

Don't misunderstand. If you only think and not feel, you can easily misunderstand this. If you are a man, you might think that this subject implies that women must overpower men. If you are a woman you might feel good to know men need work. It depends on the level of inner standing that you currently have about life and everything making up your reality. Balance must be restored. At one point in the distant past, women ruled and by "ruled" I don't mean controlling humanity.

More like leading our species. A woman or a man that is balanced when both left and right brain hemispheres function efficiently, will not hurt another person, animal or any other form of life. Furthermore, a woman would definitely not send their children to war.

Predominantly, masculinity was enforced for the purpose to bury the Goddess feminine so that those that controlled the narrative would make sure to keep humanity fighting with each other. Nowadays or in the most recent past where women fought/fight each other, happened/happens as a result of the controllers manipulating both men and women, resulting in the destruction of the family nucleus.

The women's movement that happened over 100 years ago for equal rights was simply to get women to work. The government took 50% more taxes, and the state would raise their children for them in the form of the education/ indoctrination system.

Women were duped just as men were for many thousands of years. Family is (should be) the most important thing in our society. You must look within and balance both feminine and masculine aspects in you. Men are not superior to women and vice versa. It's what the controllers want us to think so we can fight amongst each other.

WOMEN: Get your power back. Nurture men. They must protect you, and they have to protect you, not the government.

YOU ARE QUEENS

A WORD TO WOMEN:

You are a Goddess who emerges from deep within yourself. You are a woman who has honestly explored your darkness and learned to celebrate your light. You are a woman who is able to rise (Footnote #6) in love with the magnificent possibilities within you. You are a woman who knows of the magic and the mysterious places inside you. The sacred places that can nurture your soul and make you whole. You are a woman who radiates Light. You are magnetic and MAGNIFICENT.

Sexual intercourse is a sacred and spiritual act. You are giving someone else permission to enter (inter) the (course) way of your spirit. You have no control of what they might obtain or what residues they might leave behind. Choose your partner wisely. DO NOT say "*other half*" because there's no such thing as the other. You are "whole". All it takes is one single time for them to take up residency in your temple. You are immensely powerful. You have been chosen by God to be the portal between the spiritual realm and the physical one.

Be wise about who you open portals with. Sex is a spiritual transfer of energy so powerful that you can open a portal from the spirit world into the physical realm. When you (both genders) have an orgasm, you open a portal between this and the spiritual realm. The spiritual realm, just like our physical one, has good and bad spirits/entities - light and dark ones.

It is particularly important to know the difference between when you open portals by having an intercourse with someone you genuinely care and love (they must feel the same toward you) or when you open portals with someone that doesn't have your best interest in mind. Portals open also when you watch adult content.

If you innerstand that in the quantum field everything can be transferred instantaneously within this physical realm or between physical and metaphysical realm, then you can easily see that if the adult content was created with the intention to drain/suck your energy (they all are) and destroy your brain grey matter, then it will be transferred to you, even if the adult content is watched on a screen. When you watch something on a screen, do you have a chemical reaction? Yes, you do.

Thoughts, emotions and all chemical reactions are energy. Just as you feel chemical reaction by watching something, you will also have a reaction on an energetic level. Energy transfer is very real.

Be very mindful of who you let within your energetic chamber. When having a sexual act with someone, you revive that person's trauma because since the act itself is a release of energy, you will receive any negative energy that person has. You will heal that person to a certain point, but you will make yourself sick in return.

Your sickness will be even worse when that other person's health habits are below standard. If that person consumes meat regularly, alcohol, processed food or low vibrational content such as mind control programs etc, then his/her auric field is compromised and it is guaranteed that low vibrational entities have taken hold of his/her temple that has crumbled.

You will then attract those entities into your temple whether or not you have sexual intercourse with that person. As long as you are within that person's auric field, his low vibrational entities that have taken hold of him, will be like a magnet to you if you are not healed or if you have emotional and mental trauma.

Be mindful who you hang around with. If you are the one with the damaged auric field then you can repair it by eating healthy, exercising, fasting and meditating. Protect your portals. Your mind is a portal also. Be your own portal keeper. Hold the key to the portal tight. You are the only force on this planet powerful enough to navigate the unborn spirit into this planet. How amazing is that? Don't take your birthing process for granted.

Many women wish to not have brought life to their children. They can't grasp the magnificent intelligent design that they are. Many thousands of years ago, humanity lived in a world of Gods and Goddesses. Today we live in a world solely of Gods. Women in most cultures have been stripped of their spiritual power. That is ending. Feminine energy is coming back.

There are not going to be any more wars. Humanity will thrive. Families will be united. Men and women will respect and love everyone unconditionally as we were originally designed to.

Men who abstain from casual sex, pornography and masturbation, raise the vibration of the collective as a whole.. When you (men) stop entertaining lust, sex indulgence and other carnal pleasures, you become protectors of purity. Being pure, makes you the best, son, father and husband. Being pure, you make the world safer for women and children. You see other men as your brothers and you develop a greater appreciation for motherhood. Lust becomes repulsive. Virtue becomes "the new beauty." When you are pure, you will attract women because they will naturally feel comfortable around you because you don't carry the vibration/frequency of sexual perversion. When you have self-control over your body, mind and soul, you are the paragon of masculinity.

AFFIRMATIONS

- I AM the Goddess of my inner self.
- I AM the cosmic power encapsulating and balancing all energy.
- I AM at peace with everything that happened to me in the past.
- I AM being myself and I bring happiness to others.
- I control my thoughts and emotions.
- I AM lovable, healthy, positive and happy.

- I AM the Goddess of the Universe.

A WORD TO MEN:

We, as men, along with evolving ourselves, would do quite well to innerstand that the Sacred Women of this beautiful planet have been dominated, suppressed, manipulated, mistreated, disempowered, abused, neglected, silenced, and otherwise maligned for CENTURIES. These Magnificent Beings of the female persuasion are now breaking all those shackles and embracing their power and sovereignty. They carry a consensus group disdain for their long-term oppression.

Our Loving Support of their much awaited return to their Goddess Selves is needed as they find their way back to who they always were before it was stripped from them. Be patient, be flexible, and know that if you are a decent man with a good heart who cherishes her and lights her fires she will choose you. She might seem to be pulling away, but that is just her finding her crown of true Sovereignty. If you are falling short of being her choice, step it up a little. Go the extra mile, or five, or twenty. She will notice and cherish you for showing her how worthy she is to you by your efforts and actions.

Our role as men is honoring ourselves, and double honoring the finally free to be Radiant Divine Goddesses walking in our midst. Divine masculine will be feeling the strong shift in the energies. Their fear of being away from their feminine is surrounding them and they will be pushed to take physical action toward their feminine. Bad dreams, distance and longing for their divine Feminine is what is coming up and the righteous path will be clear to them.

Their Ego self will die, their intuition is going to make them take divine steps toward inner union.

You must create a personal relationship with God by looking within. I'm pretty sure the divine masculine is aware of this. Sometimes us guys need to hear it in case our Divine masculine is distorted by the confusions of this crazy world. We all need healing. Say "no more" to being separated. We both need each other. We are each other.

The Divine Masculine is moving through an important upgrade. One that will help them see through the dark fog that had consumed them since the end of 2019. Rejection wounds from the Dark Mother that block receiving will come. You will also be looking at healing in a more focused manner as inner DM (Divine Feminine) is now waking up to the Source. It is all about receiving hence forth and you will inner stand what it means to accept yourself and *heal the childhood* trauma that has sabotaged the union between the Divine Feminine and the Divine Masculine energies. Any father issues that highlight abandonment and shame will also come up for reflection. A tower moment regarding Sexuality will take place as wounds masquerading as False

Projections will collapse.

You will innerstand better who you are and you won't let Unconscious behavior in Karmic Timelines hurt you or the DF (Divine Feminine). You also may be guided to open Lines of Communications to express yourself.

YOU ARE KINGS
YOU MUST PROTECT THE QUEENS
YOU MUST BECOME STRONG AGAIN
YOU MUST CREATE FREEDOM SAFETY and PROTECTION FOR the
WOMEN AND the CHILDREN.

ΔΔΔ

CHOOSE YOUR PARTNER WISELY

Your partner (whichever gender you may be) is there to teach you to become a better person or to destroy you. Either or, it is still a "teaching". Would you rather learn the lessons within this lifetime or in the next 10, 50, or 1000 lifetimes?

If the partner is depleted of their life force then they will siphon yours during intimate encounters. A life force is depleted through negative thinking, gossiping, unhealthy eating habits, casual sex, non exercise and more. In the case of men - the main life force energy that they lose/waste is "*semen*". That's why adult content has become a big problem in the modern world. Watching that kind of content, it robs the life (life force) out of both women and men. Not just adult content, but everywhere there is sexualization, such as movies, magazines, online etc.

Semen retention is a must for a man to become strong mentally, emotionally, and spiritually. Retention for men, is a blessing. Not just for them but also for women. In my book "**BODY MIND SOUL: AS YOU BELIEVE SO SHALL IT BE**". I wrote a chapter about this very important subject. The chapter name is "*Orgasming without ejaculating-Semen Retention*".

Retaining is the key (one of them) to create a stronger male species. A strong male will protect women. Just like women are the key in nurturing the fragile men. There are many divorces and break ups between the two sexes in recent decades. WHY IS THAT? That is because hidden forces don't want the man and woman to be united.

When we are united and resonate in high frequency, we are unstoppable. We become one with the Creator. We create realities at will. We cannot manifest heaven on Earth with a weak species. A species that is sexually driven is a species that is confused and doesn't know the purpose of living. Sex must be treated as sacred and not as an activity. Sex in an exchange of energy. More often than not it is lopsided. It is an unbalanced exchange of energy. A relationship based on sex is vampiric. It is even worse than someone drinking your blood. They drain your energy and inject into you their traumatic wounded diseases destroying you spiritually, emotionally, and mentally. This takes time to recover, if you recover at all.

> *A person that stays with you mostly for sex, denies that the sex is parasitic as it is painful for them because they need to feed off of your energetic field or life force to sustain their shallow parasitic selves.*

You owe it to yourself to do a parasitic cleanse. Both a physical and an energetic cleanse. Get rid of those kind of people feeding off of you sexually. They will find another one to leech off of until they will *one way or another* get healed. Their healing will begin to offer positive healing energy back instead of sucking it out of other people. Growth in a relationship happens when both partners heal each other and when both partners water and not draining each other. You cannot grow in the presence of someone that refuses to heal.

You are in no way responsible to heal them if they themselves are not willing to put the effort in healing their wounded child within. Casual sex or the dating scene is full of unhealed people with internal energy blockages. They will parasite off of your energy. Do not allow that for temporary sexual surface pleasure. You will be harmed by receiving their insecurities, their low self-esteem, and their past traumatic experiences/low energy. Semen retention protects their energy and makes it possible to heal themselves and you.

> *If you are a man, I greatly suggest you practice semen retention (refer to the chapter ORGASMING WITHOUT EJACULATING-SEMEN RETENTION in the book BODY MIND SOUL AS YOU BELIEVE SO SHALL IT BE.*

> *If you are a woman, do not enter in an energetic contract with a man that does not practice semen retention. A man that ejaculates for the purpose of a few seconds of pleasure, is half a man.*

Do not settle for less. This of course applies when you have realized your purpose, when you know your worth. Only then, will you have a successful relationship. A relationship doesn't necessarily have to be physical. At first, it may be energetic (before an eventual meeting in person), especially in our times when many people meet online. Online interaction is great, but it has its shortcomings. One of them is that you will be bombarded with images or texts from different people. By the time you have built a connection with someone, you will be distracted by other people's messages and that can affect your previous built up (momentum). So that is why it is very important that you speak your mind. When you are speaking your mind, you are becoming clear of your intentions. Do not say things just to be nice. The person at the other side of the screen might develop false or an imaginary connection.

Be centered,

Be grounded, Be yourself
and you will see how your life will improve every day.

"KEEP YOUR HANDS TO YOURSELF" PRACTICE ABSTINENCE

This is for both males and females. If you learn how to not lose the elixir (semen/sexual energy), then use your hands (or you feet) as much as you want. Research and you will easily find ways to achieve pleasure without wasting your most precious fluids. Do not waste your semen (or sexual energy for women too). It is your life force. Abstinence applies to both genders. When you abstain (with the exception of tantric sex) your sexual energy is not wasted. Your Kundalini energy will awaken and rise.

This creative powerful sexual energy a.k.a. the "Kundalini" will unlock all your chakras (including the pineal gland) and you will be transmuted from a dense physical enslaved being to a free spiritual force. The ideal time to practice abstinence is when the Moon is in your Sun sign. When you have an orgasm, your body is depleted of your life force since you wasted it (the energy) externally. This means that you must conserve the sexual energy for longer than the days when the Moon is in your zodiac/Sun sign. For more on this subject check the book *GAIN WISDOM THROUGH PRACTICED KNOWLEDGE by RIMIAS K. NEO*

Why do you think adult content is rampant and free everywhere? It is to entice people to waste their life force. Without your life force you are a robot. By not wasting your sexual energy/life force, your physical, mental, emotional and spiritual life will improve tenfold. Keeping this *"God-like"* elixir inside of you through abstinence, can also slow the aging process. It's a good "all-around" medicine for your whole being. As Friedrich Nietzsche said.

"The reabsorption of semen by the blood is the strongest nourishment and, perhaps more than any other factor, it prompts the stimulus of power, the unrest of all forces toward the overcoming of resistances,

the thirst for contradiction and resistance. The feeling of power has
so far mounted highest in abstinent Priests and hermits (for example,
among the Brahmans)"

Abstinence not only improves your eyesight but everything physical and metaphysical. This applies to both men and women unless you have to procreate or you have a relationship with someone of a high frequency. Blindness such as long or short-sighted vision are simply congestion in the eyes, due to build up mucus. This can be fixed through abstinence. Well, it goes without saying that you must also eat healthy, fast, sun gaze, ground yourself, meditate etc. In the book **Rebuild Yourself From Within** by J.J. and TAMO, the authors say this about the consequences of semen/life force loss from masturbation or conventional sex:

Eminent doctors of the west say that various kinds of diseases arise from the loss of semen, particularly in young age. There appear boils on the body, acne or eruptions on the face, blue lines around the eyes, absence of beard, sunken eyes, pale face with anaemia, loss of memory, loss of eye-sightedness, discharge of semen along with urine, enlargement of the testes, pain in the testes, debility, drowsiness, laziness, gloominess, palpitation of the heart, dyspnoea or difficulty in breathing, phthisis, pain in the back, loins, head and joints, weak kidneys, passing urine in sleep, fickle-mindedness, lack of thinking power, bad dreams, wet dreams and restlessness of mind.

Mark carefully the evil after-effects that follow the loss of seminal energy! Persons are physically, mentally and morally debilitated by wasting the seminal power on so many occasions for nothing. The body and mind refuse to work energetically. There is a physical and mental lethargy. You experience much exhaustion and weakness. The addiction has had profound consequences on our well-being. We have personally experienced discomfort in the elbows, knees, and lower back, along with feelings of depression, brain fog, and low self-esteem. Moreover, it has caused a lack of motivation, confidence, and determination. It has also stifled our creativity and stripped away our spiritual abilities.

Additionally, it has resulted in a loss of libido, heightened anxiety, and extreme fatigue. Furthermore, it has impacted our ability to concentrate, our strength, and our focus. Lastly, every ejaculation, whether through masturbation or conventional sex, has made us feel three times older than our actual age.

20

DOLPHINS ARE THE BEST MIDWIVES

A Russian male midwife named Igor Charkovsky has been involved in underwater birthing for a long time. He has assisted with over 20,000 underwater births. In 1979 he began experiments with dolphins and children. His first daughter, one of the first to be born underwater, was in her twenties when the following incident took place. Charkovski and his team had taken a woman to the Mediterranean Sea for an underwater birth.

They were sitting there prepared for the birth with the woman lying in water two feet deep. A few dolphins approached and pushed everybody away proceeding to take over. The dolphins scanned up and down her body (with sonar?) which relaxed the woman and unborn child. She then gave birth with no pain or fear.

It was a phenomenal experience. All the midwives were shocked. The experience with underwater birthing began a new practice of using dolphins as midwives. For some reason dolphins are attracted to pregnant women and children. There's something about the sonar that dolphins project at the time of birth that seems to relax both the mother and child. Dolphins have preferences to humans.

Maybe at one point we were dolphins. You may think this is nonsense and ridiculous because you are assuming that we evolved from dolphins. That is not how it happened. We must go beyond the 5 senses of reality to grasp some concepts. By the end of the book, you should consider anything is possible if and when you innerstand both sides of the coin- Physical and metaphysical. Let's go back to the dolphins having preferences to humans. If you go swimming with dolphins and there are children around, the dolphins will gravitate towards the children first. If there are no children, they will go to women. If there are no women, they go to men. If there's a woman who is pregnant then everyone else can forget it. She gets their total attention. The little incoming baby is the greatest happiness for all. Which is something all humans MUST innerstand.

This "Dolphin midwifery" practice has produced super children.

Extraordinary children. From all the research being done so far, not one of those children has an IQ under 150 (genius level) and they have extremely stable emotional bodies and extremely strong physical bodies. Water is becoming their natural environment. Dolphins, just like any other species, have a purpose here, not just for the ecosystem but also related specifically to us. There is ample evidence that humans once had a much more intrinsic connection with water.

Charkovsky believes that man's close affinity with aquatic animals can be explained by our common origin in water based on our mammalian history. In the book THE AQUATIC APE, Elaine Morgan gives a fascinating account of the aquatic theory of evolution. According to Morgan, our aquatic affinity goes back millions of years to the Pliocene age, when our ape ancestors (Footnote #7) lived a semi-aquatic life on the coastline to escape the extreme heat which occurred due to climatic change.

By wading in the sea, our ancestors began to walk upright and lost their body hair and developed a layer of subcutaneous fat like other aquatic mammals, to protect them from the cooler temperatures of the water. Today, we still have this layer of subcutaneous fat. As many people are aware of, dolphins can also help heal people with mental and psychological problems. Drunvalo Melchizedek in his book *The ancient secret of the flower of life-volume 1*, describes a time where he spent time with a woman who was an assistant of Charkovsky in Russia. She had brought back many films that were taken during these births.

As Melchizedek writes, he watched two movies of two different women giving birth who not only were not in pain, but were having orgasms (while giving birth to their children) lasting twenty minutes. It was a total pleasure. It's how it's supposed to be. It simply makes sense, and these women were proving it. There are also videos where babies sleep on the bottom of swimming pools in Russia.

They literally sleep underwater on the bottom of the pool and roughly every ten minutes while asleep they would rise to the surface, roll their faces over, take a breath, go back down and settle on the bottom again. Those kids live in the water. That's their home. They're being given a name, almost like they're a different species. People are calling them "homodolphins". Water is becoming their natural medium, and all of them are extremely intelligent. The possibility of having dolphins around while giving birth underwater is truly a gift. It is a healthy trend the way that many countries are allowing this new way of birth. Or should I say it is a new way because we are stuck in the old unnatural distorted way.

Many countries are practicing this underwater birthing process such as in the U.S.A, New Zealand, Australia and a few other places. The more women see other women not in pain, they are going to want to do it. Now, at least in the developed countries as far as I know, to relieve pain during labor, women request an epidural. The goal of an epidural is to provide analgesia, or pain relief, rather than anesthesia, which leads to a total lack of feeling. An epidural blocks the nerve impulses from the lower spinal segments. This results in a decreased sensation in the lower half of the body. While this may sound good, because it alleviates strong pain, it has side effects. The most dangerous side effect is that you might get paralyzed if the needle pinches a nerve in your spine. It is exceedingly rare that it might happen, but it does happen. This is not to scare you, but better being aware of the many side effects that you may have. Consider going through the underwater birthing process.

If I was a woman and if I didn't know any better, I would have chosen the epidural injection in a heartbeat. In the end, it is up to you if you want to choose dolphins, epidural injection or the old fashion/ natural way. Even if you are someone that is not going to have any more children, it is moral and logical to mention to other women the best natural way to give birth. Dolphins are your friends. They may be " YOU " from an extreme but optimal parallel timeline. Dolphins are a deeply knowledgeable species and they know pretty much everything, just as you also know everything.

You just don't remember. One day you will remember everything, as long as you don't reject what you cannot innerstand.

Dolphins know who or what created everything (the Universe). For example, dolphins may know who built "**THE MOON**"

21

WHO CONTROLS THE MOON ?

" My gravest secret is that I really did fake the moon landing. On Venus." -Richard Nixon

Before our reality was hijacked, the planet Saturn did not have any rings. How does our moon fit into this? The moon is a satellite that picks up energetic information from Saturn's broadcasting grid. The moon then receives this information and redirects it to the Earth where the transmissions are then received by the Earth's crystal core. The crystal core then retransmits these vibratory signals to the inhabitants on the planet, which affects our consciousness. The relationship between Saturn and our moon is coherent.

The moon's 29.5 cycles a day keeps us hormonally tied to the tiny, repeated cycles and the 29-and-a-half-year cycle of Saturn. This locks us into societal structures that aren't visible to the naked eye. The moon is simply a supercomputer. A satellite that was constructed outside of Earth's atmosphere as a monitoring and mediating device. I suggest you watch the movie the Truman Show.

The movie tells us that the moon is a satellite and that it creates our reality. There are countless ancient stories from the Zulus, Colombians and many other aboriginals all over the Earth who all tell tales of a time where the moon did not exist in our skies. These people were known as the "Pro Selene" , which translates to - *'Those who were before the Moon'*.

Our moon was not designed for malicious purposes, but to aid in speeding up human's evolutionary journey. When the energy is picked up by the satellite as positive, the signal projected to the Earth can be one of a loving nature. If that signal is hacked, you can choose the vibration you want to emit. The reptilians knew this was an antenna that could suppress our Light which could then block the kundalini from awakening inside of us through a strong and negative frequency. There are many theories as to how the moon came to be. The mainstream theory is that the infant Earth was blasted by an object more massive than Mars.

During that collision, a big chunk of Earth came off which formed the moon called the Big Whack theory. Few scientists say that the moon doesn't exist. They say that it is easier to explain its non-existence than its actual existence. The Reptilians keep humanity manipulated through this energy of Saturn. The crystals used to create broadcasting systems come from their advanced technology within their Reptilian alliance.

They use Saturn as their master control center. Some argue that Saturn's rings were created by debris from a disintegrated moon. However, this cannot explain how it would be possible to create a ring 3.7 million miles away from Saturn that could hold a billion Earths combined. Saturn gets its name from Satan.

The worship of Satan (Saturn) comes from mind control over our planet. Saturn creates an awfully specific firewall within our holographic reality, which limits us to only a tiny minuscule spectrum of light. Over 99.99% of our reality is shielded from us through this false energetic grid. Six-six-six comes from our carbon-based DNA which has six protons, six neurons and six electrons. 666 numbers also come from Saturn's 6-sided hexagon.

This is why the abbreviated term ' hex ' is represented as a spell or witchcraft as it emulates the trickery and illusion of the Saturn matrix. The number also comes from the Masonic magic square of Saturn.

This hexagon shape is formed on the top of Saturn's north pole. It generates this particular formation because of the specific energy it radiates. It radiates two and a half times more energy than it receives from the Sun. The hexagon rotates in sync with Saturn's recorded radio emissions, which when you translate these sound vibrations into semantics, the sound waves create the projection of the six-pointed star. On the south pole of Saturn there is a permanent eye storm, which is representative of the 'all seeing eye' which you see in the Illuminati or Cabal symbol.

The scientists who call a lot of our DNA 'junk', are just brainwashing us with the Saturn satanic agenda. They are trying hard to convince us that our so-called junk genetics need to be changed and that there is technology available to alter our biology for our own benefit. These genes that they call junk are not useless. They just stay dormant through the programming of the matrix.

If we can bust out of the Reptilian consciousness through Love and Light, then these genetics will get activated to the strongest potential. It is our choice whether these get switched on or not through our thoughts, beliefs and actions. Do not fall victim to the mainstream narrative that you need to be upgraded so that you can become a more useful part of society. When you become Light, you restore your genetics back to the real YOU. The essence of your core, your soul being.

Only then, with enough Light can you break through the firewall of the matrix and out of the control of Lucifer's influence. Don't get sucked into the drama. Keep vibrating high and send Love and Light to all. The Moon is most likely a false light in which we don't know who exactly controls it. At one point it was being controlled by the Archons up to a few years ago, I think.

At another point in time it was controlled by a benevolent species. There are conflicting theories. If two theories are conflicting, that does not mean one of them is a lie. Both theories could be true. The question is the timing of the theories. One theory originated thousands of years ago while the other could be recent. Believing one over the other is simply a matter of how much you have researched them, and you might lean toward one or the other.

The Moon is not bad. Many people perform rituals, especially when there is a full moon. Anything can be bad or good depending on your focus. Since we already know beyond a doubt that we create what we think, we let our thoughts dictate the materialization of anything life brings us. The malevolent species that supposedly control the moon direct their energetic mind control signal on us. Earth is the stage. Could the Moon be a projector? Watch the movie *The Truman Show*.

22

DO YOU KNOW YOUR POTENTIAL ?

"The big challenge is to become all that you have the possibility of becoming. You cannot believe what it does to the human spirit to maximize your human potential and stretch yourself to the limits."

-JIM ROHN

Whenever someone repeatedly attacks your confidence and self-esteem, they are quite aware of your potential. It has happened to me on a regular basis. I know and fully innerstand my potential and show it when needed and as a result, it has triggered and angered lots of people. Not showing it as in to 'show off' but as in expressing myself in an honest, powerful, self-assured and determined way.

I have had people try to damage my reputation and productivity at all places that I have worked since I was a teenager and outside of the workplaces. They only destroyed themselves in the end. There is a saying: "He who becomes successful by putting people down, destruction awaits him at the gate of his success". The more truthful you can be, the more people you will lose. Well, you can't lose them if their presence was only to put you down or profit from your potential.

They will weed themselves out. **The friends that you gain by being truthful, will be the true friends you can truly trust, who will not stab you in the back**. Sometimes in this book I speak in the 1st person to explain certain situations about me and it's not about rambling about my personal life. It's to show you how I have been through certain situations and how those situations helped me to grow.

Picture yourself in those situations or other similar situations when people treat you a certain way. You can compare them and find a solution so you won't be taken advantage of by people. No matter how many situations and people you have to go through in life, it comes down to one thing. You MUST love yourself. There is no other choice. Your life will be a disaster if you don't love yourself. It doesn't matter how much money you have. If you are empty in your heart, your life is forfeit.

At one point while I was in the middle of writing this book, someone asked what the book was about. I told him the message that I was trying to portray through this book and that person said: *"I can also write a book with the same message"*, and I told him, *"Yes, you can, as a matter of fact, anyone can but why dont YOU"*? He didn't answer. I knew the answer and he knew I knew the answer. The answer was that he and many others don't have the determination and dedication to see it through to completion. Anything in life requires determination and strong will. Otherwise you might self-sabotage your precious life in a cruel and immobilizing way. Any famous philosopher, public figure or artist is no different than you or anyone else in their core self.

What makes you who you are, is your qualities such as determination, high self-esteem and powerful thinking and feeling abilities. Many people have great ideas to accomplish everything their hearts desire, but they lack the will to start a project. They also lack the determination to see through to completion their projects, plans or ideas. And so, their dreams remain just that, "dreams". Their dreams don't materialize because the missing ingredients (qualities) are absent. Not that they are absent per se, it's that they are buried under the emotional and mental conditioning they had to endure throughout their life.

Being determined doesn't necessarily mean being an artist, becoming an author or anything that would put you higher than the majority. Being an artist or a writer or anything else, doesn't make you a better person. Just as I am not any better than you, just because I wrote this book. You too can become anything you want. My role as an author is to help you awaken from within. I don't have more powers than you. It's all about sheer will, determination and discipline. When you have these three you can achieve anything you desire.

Determined can also mean being a role model as a father, a mother, a friend or anything you want to be that would contribute to the betterment of your life and those that you come in contact with. You have to unlearn everything you have been programmed to falsely beLIEve since birth. The programming includes beliefs acquired from the education (actually *indoctrination*) system, parents and the society in general.

That glitch (opinions, beliefs and separation from the real SELF), that software no longer serves you if you want to live in a world where all things are within your reach, where all things are possible. You have that power. Nobody can take that away from you. Anything you truly ask for, in prayer or meditation you can believe that you have received it and it will be yours.

Breathe deeply and hold your breath for 5 seconds, release slowly and repeat after me, *I AM powerful, I AM invincible, I AM eternal, My potential is unlimited.* If you learn to observe and appreciate things for what they are, without the need to control them by letting them be, you will reside in the circle. In the center of the Universe. You become your own master.

AFFIRMATIONS.

- My potential is unlimited.
- I AM strong emotionally, physically and mentally.
- I don't need to be compared to anyone.
- My inner power radiated both inwards and out wards.
- I strive to reach maximum potential every day.
- My intentions are realized through my genuine potential.
- I have the unlimited ability to conquer any challenge.

Your eyes are to see externally, but your third eye (pineal gland) is the spiritual eye. Your 3rd eye/pineal gland is your 6th sense/intuition.

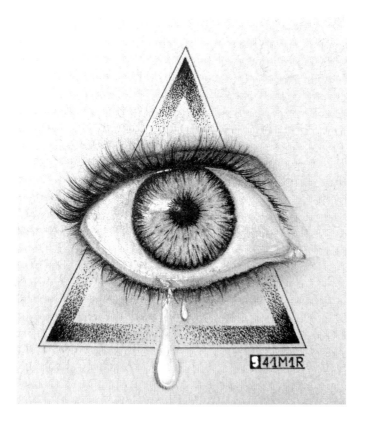

Work on decalcifying your pineal gland, the seat of your soul, the bridge between the physical and the metaphysical. The one eye is the pineal gland. The powers that be twist all symbols so they (the symbols) can be seen as evil. That way people won't look into them and find the true meaning of the symbols. Within you, there is God/Creator. It's what religion has always kept from you. They talk about God but they don't tell you where God actually is. You don't need anyone to tell you, because you are a God/ Goddess.

23

DETACHED OBSERVER

"The observer is the observed "- Jiddu Krishnamurti

What is a detached observer? Being a detached observer is when you can place yourself in a situation whether it be with coworkers, friends, family or a lover, and you are able to look at the bigger picture from a perspective of non-attachment and observation. This requires great trust and confidence. You must trust and be confident that you can enter this situation and remain the observer. Once you become emotionally involved, you are no longer an observer, you are now the experiencer. Whenever you recall a situation, habit or relationship that requires your attention, I suggest that you go into it with the intention of not being emotionally attached to anything but to become an observer.

> *Once you realize that a moment requires your attention is to soon occur, for you can sense when you are about to react emotionally, say to yourself – "I intend to only observe in this moment, I choose to not react, but watch, listen and observe." Then, when any emotional triggering moment arises, you must focus on only observing it.*

This means listening carefully to all parties involved, paying close attention to the tone of their voice, body language and what they are communicating. Observe what feelings are involved for all parties. Observe what feelings and thoughts may be arising within yourself. It is ok for you to have thoughts and feelings arise, but you must stay detached from them and not react to them.

You must only observe your thoughts, feelings and emotions and not react to them. It is once you react that you are no longer the observer. Then, if necessary, you must also communicate from this place of observation. Always do this so you can remain in a place of neutrality during these moments. You are then able to leave it with much more information than if you become emotionally involved. You can then gather all the information related to a situation, then process it with clarity and inner standing. This allows you to learn and innerstand whether it is serving you to continue in this way, or if there needs to be any changes. There are far too many outcomes to explain here, but I will give an overall view on how you can navigate this process. Once you have been the observer, you will easily know how it feels to be involved with whatever it may be. You can see instead of experience, all the pros and cons that arise. This means you can clearly evaluate the information gathered; then decide how you must proceed. It is when you continue being emotionally involved, that your vision is foggy, and you struggle to gain clarity. Because the emotions are directly involved, they sway your consciousness back and forth and make it much harder to think clearly or make rational decisions.

Once you have gathered the necessary information, you can then ask yourself questions such as – "Does this person have my best interests at hand?". "Are they helping me grow?". "Do I feel fulfilled and happy?". "Is this healthy for my body, mind and spirit?". Once you receive the answers to these questions, you must then evaluate them and then take the necessary steps.

If you have situations that keep arising in your life that you struggle to gain clarity around, this tool is the solution. You may not become the observer on your first attempt, but that's ok. This teaches neutrality. Neutrality does not simply occur in an instant. It requires practice and discipline.

But like everything else in your life, practice makes perfect. The less emotionally attached you become, the more you observe and gather information. The greater is the clarity you gain and the clearer your path to enlightenment (**In-Light-Ment**) becomes.

AFFIRMATIONS

- I observe and don't get emotionally invested.
- I consciously commit to observation and detachment.
- My life revolves through a state of engaged detach ment.
- I embrace observational detachment and I choose emotional and mental clarity.
- I choose to be free from good and bad opinions of others.
- I AM focusing on myself and I detach from external noises.

- I AM a detached observer and I don't let myself get distracted by things that happen or things that WILL happen because it is always NOW o' clock.

24

IT IS "NOW" O' CLOCK

"No matter how much energy you waste in memories and imagination, the only thing that matters is NOW" - S.K

The past is just previous present moments and the future is awaiting present moments. Therefore, what matters is that there are only present moments. Don't look at the time if you don't have to do anything based on time. It will make you anxious. There is no point in wasting energy that you will not get back. You were born with a full battery. Every time you spend energy on things that don't benefit your overall well-being, the power of the battery empties. Do you realize how many times throughout life you unnecessarily waste your battery?

Thousands of times. We could live for hundreds of years if we were conscious of every thought and action during our everyday life. We are distracted with memories and imagination of an unknown future outcome. And in the meantime, we lose the present, **we lose what we can never, ever get back.**

Looking at things and enjoying them in the moment is way better than taking pictures or videos of everything for viewing at a later moment.

Many people say, *"One day I will do that, or eventually I will get into this or that".* That is the procrastinator's trait.

If you want to do something, start Now. Today is the day. Tomorrow never comes. You are blessed as soon as you were created by and from the Divine Source. Every day is a new beginning.

If the new day doesn't bring you upliftment and peace, then you are living in the past through your memories or in the future through your imagination. Time and space happen all at once. Time doesn't move forward or back. Time is a fixed nature. Time is an interesting subject.

Time can work in your favour or not.
Time can reward or punish you.
Time can be your enemy or friend.
Time can kill you or give you life.

Your perceptions and emotions dictate whether time favours you or not. Time simply reflects your state of mind. Time will keep ticking no matter the choices you make in life. Time does not have any feelings. Time doesn't judge. Time is not racist. By being in the present, time will cease to exist. All you have is "**NOW**"

PHANTOM TIME THEORY

A little known German historian, writer, and publisher Heribert Illig is perhaps one of the most eccentric conspiracy theorists out there. He developed the PTT (Phantom Time Theory) which says that the years AD614 through 911, is a period commonly known in standard history as the Early Middle Ages and it never happened.

Illig says that the Middle Ages, a period that includes the collapse of the Roman, the rise of Islam, the rise (and fall) of the Byzantine Empire, and the Viking Age, among other fundamental epochs, didn't happen. That period of time was at some point made up by the academic establishment through a series of blunders and a heavy reliance on antique documents, which he believes are unreliable. Illig says that the current year isn't 2014(he said this 7 years ago), but rather 1739, some 273 years out of date.

The basis of his theory is the discrepancies seen in the Julian calendar introduced by Julius Caesar. It was long known to introduce a discrepancy from the tropical year of around one day for each century that the calendar was in use. By the time the Gregorian calendar was introduced in AD 1582, Illig alleged that the old Julian calendar should have produced a discrepancy of thirteen days between it and the real (or tropical) calendar.

Instead, the astronomers and mathematicians working for Pope Gregory had found that the civil calendar needed to be adjusted by only ten days. From this, Illig concludes that the AD era had counted roughly three centuries which never existed.

He also cites a lack of archeological evidence for the events thought to have occurred during that time, as well as the presence of Romanesque architecture in tenth-century Europe. Why? Good question. As you may imagine, however, the historical community does not support Illig's theory . I wonder why they don't support his theory. (It's a rhetorical question, you may guess the "why").

Conspiracy theories and their proponents often get ridiculed as crackpots, weirdos, nut jobs, etcetera. While some of them might be ridiculous, it benefits no one to dismiss their ideas out of hand without first examining the evidence to determine if there might be some truth to it. Rational, logical examination, followed by calm and open discourse is the only way to navigate the muddy waters. There is so much we do not know. No matter what, don't lose grip of the present. Trust the magic of new beginnings.

Don't get caught in yesterday's history or tomorrow's mystery. The present moment is a gift. That is what you should focus on. Anytime you catch yourself overthinking about the past or the future, breathe consciously to bring yourself in the present.

Breathing consciously with the diaphragm is the ideal remedy to suffering under the mighty imaginary weapon called "TIME"

*Every breath you take will dictate the path to enlightment or destruction. Diaphragmatic breathing is the secret. When you breathe consciously, you are in the moment. When you are in the moment, **time** does not exist.*

25

TIME IS AN ILLUSION

"Time is only an illusion produced by the succession of our states of consciousness as we travel through eternal duration, and it does not exist where no consciousness exists in which the illusion can be produced; but "lies asleep" - H. P. Blavatsky

Time doesn't exist, clocks do. Time is just an agreed upon construct. We have taken distance (one rotation of the Earth, and one orbit of the Sun), divided it up into segments and then give those segments labels. While it has it's uses, we have been programmed to live our lives by this construct as if it were real. We have confused our shared construct with something that is tangible and thus have become its slave.

Time is merely a figment of our limited perception of our reality. Everything that has happened in the past, or that will happen in the future, is technically happening simultaneously right now. When a hypnosis technique is used to tap into past lives, it's actually tapping into a parallel life. After all, how could it be a version of you in the past if you are still able to communicate with them (*beings from the other side of the physical life*) now? That is because it's not the past. That version of you, currently still exists in another reality. It exists in a parallel life or alternate timeline. I can confirm 100% that time is an illusion. Since I stopped working for a CORPoration, time stopped for me. I don't know what time is, and I don't know what day it is. I don't have to set the alarm to get up at a certain time, I don't have to look at the clock when it's time to leave the house. I don't have to look at the clock in the car to see if I will get there on time. And many other instances where you need to know the time based on society's artificial constructed reality. I'm sure everyone has been trapped in the time mechanism in one way or another.

I innerstand that we have to work but don't take your work home. Most people that I know have lost precious time by talking about what happened at work (drama talk). They were concerned with how long it would take to go from here to there, or "I got to be there at a certain time" or worried they wouldn't make it and so on. All precious present moments thrown away for an illusion called TIME.

The same thing applies for the days of the week. I don't mean that you shouldn't work. At least minimize looking at the time. Don't be its prisoner. There is no need to rush. If you have done everything in your power then you have done what should be done.

Corporations don't care for your feelings or mental health. It is a business. They will push you as much as you will let them. Don't let time suck the life out of you. Although it takes time to go from point A to point B, you must not get caught in the illusion.

Just observe most of the day and you will see that time will fly by. I'm sure it happened at one point when you realized that time passed by quickly. That was because you were not caught in its trap. When you look at the watch, time passes slower.

Do you want to stop time? -**Kiss**.
Do you want to travel in time?-**Read**.
Do you want to escape time?**Listen to the music**.
Do you want to feel time?-**Write**.
Do you want to release time?-**Breathe**.

The grid that operates linear time is being rehabilitated. It has been under control and manipulation of the dark forces and has since been under restoration by benevolent higher forces/being. The seraphim lines (electromagnetic grid) are being hit the hardest right now as the process of the awakening of the world's population unfolds. The process can instill confusion and the inability to assess the concept of time as it passes as it once did. Some, such as I, *(just as you have also been called from within)* have been called to time "jump" and bear witness to all the souls that are being held captive within timelines that all happen simultaneously. Time folds in on itself by not being attached to man-made clocks/watches and calendars.

There are loops that keep certain agendas in place and right now these loops are being reformed and reintegrated for the souls (alcoholics, drug addicts etc.) that were most affected. This has left a stain in the soul of Gaia (Footnote #8). Hopefully, by now you know that Gaia is Earth, so I don't have to write both names again.

The best thing you can do is to practice GROUNDING (walking barefoot in nature, hug a tree etc.), heal and shift your frequency to that of LOVE and send it to her (GAIA/Earth) core. Some deep planetary healing is taking place right now as we all shift through this experience together. Even though it will manifest for each of us differently (some will awaken faster than others). You just got to roll with it. Like swimming in the ocean, there are swells and currents and the key is to flow with them and not against. If you are losing reference points as in missing a day, there is a reason for it. On one frame (moment in time) it's a day, on another it's just a dream (you feel like you live in between realities. It may feel like the memory of a dream and/or the memory of a memory of a dream. Some people are so affected by the speeding of time that it is causing a complete split in their psyche. We are all being shown to become intuitively led versus mentally or analytically. A linear time is just a construct not the reality. Time will no longer be relevant to this realm.

Linear time is getting dissolved. 'Time' is free yet it is priceless as far as our current constructed reality goes. You can use it but if you think you can own it, you are greatly mistaken. You can spend it as you wish but you won't be able to keep it.

<u>TIME IS AN ILLUSION, LOVING YOURSELF AND
OTHERS IS NOT AN ILLUSION.</u>

AFFIRMATIONS

- Time is a useless construct.
- I can do everything without being slowed down by artificial constructs.
- Time misspent is not lived but lost.
- It is only a little gleam of time between two eternities.
- Tides and time won't wait for me, either I observe it or use it wisely.
- If I put the illusion to good use, at least I will use it with the right people.
- I define myself the way I spend my precious time.

26

LOVE YOURSELF

I n looking for love in our society, we are dealing with frequency issues. We live in a lower vibratory consciousness that is separated from Oneness and we beLIEve (I and many others don't) in death. We believe to be the body. There is much more to who we truly are. We are physical, emotional, mental and spiritual beings. Love is the highest frequency possible. A frequency that we call GOD (Footnote #9), Home, Divine Intelligence, the Source of everything or whatever name you want to give the Creator based on your religion or personal beliefs.

You are guided by Love all the time, you just haven't realized it yet because your real you is buried underneath the darkness you haven't fought yet. You have been taught low vibratory emotions such as hate, greed, selfishness, grudge, low-self-esteem etc.

You have been profoundly courted and seduced into the beLIEf system. Loving yourself is the best thing that can happen to you. It's a miracle. Until I realized that loving myself is the ultimate cure, I was blaming things and people for bad things that happened to me. Everything you see outside of you is a mirror from within you (within your lower mind - EGO). It's a mirror of your ego. That imposter is a blood sucking leech. You can't seek love. The only thing to seek is the barriers within yourself that you have built against it.

There is no better feeling than when you love someone unconditionally and you equally get loved back with no expectations. Love can be so powerful that anything after the real thing is dim in comparison. Life will give you many chances to succeed or fail? Instead of thinking a mistake as a failure, think of it as succeeding to how not to do it next time. It's been a few years since I fought my demons. I went to hell (I dug deep within myself) looking for the light and I did find it, but only after I tamed my emotions.

The only way to find the light is by going through darkness. We never die, we only die/expire physically. We humans call it death. Physical death is just a transition of consciousness. It's like changing clothes. There is nothing to fear. Follow your heart. The heart has wisdom. It has been proven that the heart can think, in the sense that it knows everything. It has about 40 thousand neurons. It can think/know but it is not analytical. The brain does the analytical thinking.

The heart says what it feels. When you are not feeling good, remind yourself by saying *"Love is here for me now. I just have to allow it, open to it and reach for it."* You will discover that there is joy in your life and you will focus on the good aspects. It's within you where it always was. You don't seek it. Just clear the mind and heart from outside noise and love will appear.

Soft-hearted people are not weak in fact quite the opposite. Practicing kindness may not always be easy and it may sometimes leave us feeling hurt and let down. However, it is an act of great courage and strength to choose kindness over our own selfish needs and desires. Love is good/God. It is a divine feeling. However, it must not be an attachment. If there is no love, you'll suffer. I AM referring to both normal love toward another person and unconditional love toward all life. Give what you want, give what you need and then you will receive back what you have given out. Anything you desire you can receive/have it, but only when you live in the love/vibration as if you already have what you desire. You cannot give what you don't have unless you love yourself first unconditionally. Love is the most powerful and mystical force in the Universe.

Love is the primal and universal psychic energy. Love is a sacred reserve of energy. It is like the blood of spiritual evolution. Don't hope. Hope is a term used for the lazy side of desire. Get to work (working toward your rebirth), meditate and clear your mind from others telling you to be a version of you they created in their mind/reality.

Look within, it's where all answers are. Love yourself and everyone. It takes time but the rewards are amazing. Time heals everything, Time is Love's best friend.

AFFIRMATIONS

- Loving myself is the best gift I can ever have.

- Divine intelligence gave me the power to Love.

- I love solitude because it is the only way to realize

self-love.

- The healthy relationship is between two people that have innerstood self-love.

- I remember who I truly AM therefore self-love is natural.

- I AM the person that I will spend the rest of my life with therefore to love myself means to honor the eternal relation between me and myself.

- I rise in love with myself and this is the main ingredient to happiness.

<u>27</u>

"TIME" - IS LOVE'S BEST FRIEND

Below we have a beautiful story about Love and it's best friend TIME. Once upon a time, there was an island where all the feelings lived. Happiness, Sadness, Knowledge and all of the others including Love. One day it was announced that the island would sink so all constructed (Sadness, Knowledge, Happiness etc.) boats left. Except for Love. Love was the only one who stayed. Love wanted to hold out until the last possible moment. When the island had almost sunk, Love decided to ask for help. Richness was passing by Love in a grand boat. Love said,

Richness, can you take me with you? **Richness answered;** *"No, I can't. There is a lot of gold and silver in my Boat. There is no room for you".*

Love decided to ask Vanity who was also passing by in a beautiful Vessel.

"Vanity, please help me!" "I can't help you, Love .You are all wet and might damage my boat."

Vanity answered. Sadness was close by so Love asked:

"Sadness, let me go with you. "Oh, Love, I am sad so I have to be by myself!

Happiness passed by Love too but she was so happy that she didn't even hear when Love called to her. Suddenly there was a voice.

"Come Love, I will take you."

It was an elder. So blessed and overjoyed, Love forgot to ask the elder where they were going. When they arrived at dry land, the elder went her own way. Realizing how much was owed to the elder, Love asked Knowledge, who was another elder.

"Who helped me?" " It was Time," Knowledge answered. " Time?" asked Love. " But why did Time help me?"

Knowledge smiled and with deep wisdom answered.

"Only Time is capable of inner standing how valuable Love is"

Give it time and everything will be answered in time.

**Use time to your advantage or else
you will be destroyed by it.**

28

RESPECT YOUR TEMPLE

"If you are not your own doctor, you are a fool" -Hippocrates

"Everyone has a doctor in him or her. We just must help it in its work. The natural healing force within each one of us is the greatest force in getting well. Our food should be our medicine. Our medicine should be our food. But to eat when you are sick, is to feed your sickness" - Hippocrates 460 BC

Your body is your temple. You wouldn't want to destroy it, would you? With those words the famous naturopathic physician Hippocrates (Footnote #10) let us know that we can easily be our own doctors. Food is the most abused anxiety drug. Fasting is the most forgotten cure and exercise is the most underused antidepressant. Sugar/coffee/cigarettes/alcohol and prescription medications are the most abused legal drugs in our society. Would you pick these poisons or would you prefer they picked you?

The difference is one choice is conscious and the other is not. These poisons a.k.a *"legal drugs"* keep people sedated when consumed regularly. There is an exception in the case of coffee and cigarettes. Smoking doesn't keep you sedated. It just harms you primarily physically. At the time of this writing, I haven't drank coffee in 4 months. I tested myself to see if there was an improvement and there was. I AM clearer minded, more focused and more organized. You are both the poison and the cure, you decide how your life will go, toward a cliff, a bricked wall or toward a grassy/flowery horizon.

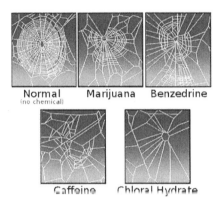

Normal   Marijuana   Benzedrine
(no chemical)

Caffeine   Chloral Hydrate

In the book **YOU ARE THE ONE** by Pine G. Land the author mentioned a great experiment that was done about coffee. She says:

There was an experiment done where some scientists gave different kinds of drugs (Caffeine, Marijuana, Benzedrine etc.) to spiders. The spider they gave coffee to, was the worst at building spiderweb. Which proves that coffee affected the spider's brain. Sugar and alcohol are the worst to be consumed because they consume you and not the other way around. While smoking and drinking coffee can mostly be bad for your physical health, sugar and alcohol can and will destroy your mental health. If medicine worked, you wouldn't need to refill your prescription.

Your prescription medicine is only suppressing the symptoms of your illness not curing it. There is no profit in the cure.

Alcohol is one of the consumptions that destroys families. When you drink alcohol, you are signing into an energetic CONtract to let the spirit of alcohol (a negative thought pattern of energy) have control over your mind.

One drop to the lips and you are drinking poison for your mind. Many people feel suicidal after drinking alcohol, some feel angry, some are more violent, some lonely and some feel superior or falsely enlightened above others. The thought pattern is always different and more negative even when joking after consuming alcohol. The jokes become sarcastic, rude or negative toward a certain person through superiority of oneself. Your thought patterns change. When you drink alcohol, check yourself about what you think, what you do and how you feel the days afterwards. Maybe get a pen and write down your thoughts and measure how different they are when you don't drink alcohol. **Alcohol is one of the best ways to lower your consciousness** and feed yourself negative thoughts and heartless energy.

Drinking alcohol opens up your body for possession.

> *Alcohol is the devil's juice. The fastest way to lower your vibration is to drink alcohol. Alcohol has been used as a weapon to keep human consciousness in a lowered state for thousands of years. By killing brain cells, it literally weakens your connection with your higher self. Figuratively and allegorically alcohol consumes you and not the other way around. Half of your lungs are on the trees (metaphorically speaking). They inhale your carbon dioxide (when you exhale), and you inhale the oxygen they produce. Without them you are an invalid.*

Try hugging a tree and feel it speak to you. You will/should feel your body vibrating. You would feel their energy if your energy was not stagnant from consuming poisons. Meat measures as alkaline on the acidic/alkaline scale but when ingested and consumed, it becomes acidic. It's the opposite for lemons which measure as acidic but when consumed, they turn into alkaline. The lower your body frequency, the more chance that you have to incarnate in the same 3d world where there are wars, famine, suffering etc.

You go ahead and eat meat, get enjoyment out of it if that's what you think it naturally gives. You may think that meat is needed for yur health because it contains vitamin B12. Just so you know, 90% of B12 supplements produced in the world are fed to livestock. Why rely on meat for B12 which is artificial. You can obtain B12 naturally from plants. In my opinion, the best plant for B12 is chlorella. I am against meat consumption. I am nobody to tell you what or what not to eat. *Refer to the **Hippocrates** quote at the very beginning of this chapter.*

I am only against consuming an animal that has been slaughtered inhumanely when is loaded with pus, antibiotics and other lab made chemicals to make the meat last longer in the shelf. Plus they inject a chemical into the meat to make it look pink and fresh when you see it on the counter. This is one reason why nobody should consume rotten flesh. The other reason why I don't personally consume dead flesh is because I don't ingest another species. If I did, I would infringe on the universal law of Love/ Harmony between the species. When I see a chicken, a cow or any other animal, I see life. I wouldn't consume it. I don't consume a life which has a nervous system. The second reason can be innerstood only when you become one with nature. Of course, if you are living in the woods and starving, you would have to kill another species (animal) to survive. Even then, you would have to give thanks to the animal providing you with life. This is not the case in our current world where you have more than enough to eat without having to slaughter an animal for food.

Soon your DNA will change as it is already changing and will change for everyone and you will hate the taste of meat because it wonn't be in sync with your DNA blueprint. Do you eat to survive or for pleasure? Answer this and you will know what needs to be done. Another thing about personal health that has numbed the logic for many is, many people compare themselves with other people such as celebrities, models, public figures or regular people in relation to their weight.

> *You don't have to be skinny to be considered healthy. You can be skinny and unhealthy or chubby and healthy. It is a problem only if it bothers you, if you genuinely don't feel good or you turn it into a drama/ big deal if someone talked about your weight. Every person based on bone density and body structure may need to be a little bit chubby or skinny. Everyone has their own ideal weight requirement, which we haven't been taught about. We have been taught to compare ourselves with others. What matters is how you feel? If you genuinely think you need to lose weight and you think that is a problem for you then do something about it but don't force your problem onto other people in the form of mental drama.*

If you are asking for help from someone, be ready to hear something that would require you to do something about it. Don't expect others to tell you what you want to hear. If you feel energetic and are active most of the time then you are fine. If you are active, eat healthy food and still fat (*I don't use political correctness words, because there is nothing wrong with using the word fat*) then the problem is in your mind. You can lose weight just by thought alone. (Refer to *reprogramming subconscious* chapter). **If you don't take time for your well-being, you will be forced to take the time for your ill-ness**.

Sungazing

Sungazing means looking directly into the sun during dawn and dusk for a few seconds at a time. Start for 3-4 seconds on the first day during dawn or dusk. It's better if you can gaze both during dawn and dusk. Increase by a couple of seconds for the next day and so on. A minute of the sun's luminosity can help you sleep better which gives you heightened energy and you can feel happier in your newfound heightened mental and physical acuity! Vitamin D is also synthesized via sunshine and it supports bone health as well as mood!

Note: *Do not look directly at the sun from after dawn till before dusk* (between **9AM** and **5PM** - depending on the season) *as it is dangerous for your eyesight.*

Don't let this scare you to the point that you might not even try sungazing. I bet if the mainstream drug dealer a.k.a. "doctor" suggested sunglasses, you would get them because you might have placed trust in the media machine. *Read again the quote at the beginning of this chapter.*

You have been conditioned to give all your senses' abilities to external things or people. I myself, sun gaze every day whenever it is sunny and not when the sun is hidden behind the chemtrail cocktail. At the time of this writing, it has been about a year since I started having problems with my sight. I would see blurry objects far away. I mentioned it to a few people and they told me to go to the optometrist and get glasses. The ones that wore glasses were the ones who suggested me to get glasses. It's like asking health advice from an obese person. I refused to take the easy way out. Well, it wouldn't be an easy way out anyway since going to the optometrist is like going to a drug dealer, I mean "Doctor". I can't help it but I don't feel like calling them by their deceptive professional name. It's not their fault. They were brainwashed at school just like the rest of us.

You might say they have helped a lot of people that had problems with their eyesight. Indeed, they have but the solution was just a patch or the answer to a problem created in advance by the same people that created the supposed solution. If the system advised people to eat healthy, exercise and think healthy, then nobody would have an eyesight problem or any other health issues. But that would mean no business for the occultist and other industries that definitely would profit from us being unhealthy. Going back to me having problems with my eyesight. I researched and found out I could do exercises for my eye muscles. Getting glasses will hinder your eye's muscles from working naturally. Hence the need to go every year to get new prescription glasses with a different number. You think you are going to fix your eyes but what you're actually doing is ruining them even further.

If the Optometrist would tell you how to fix your eyesight naturally then he would lose you as a customer. It's what you are, a customer, a bar code. When there is money to be made, life morals go out the window. The word harm is in the name 'p**HARM**acy'. Alternative medicine which is supposed to be the main healing medicine is called "holistic" - "WHOLE"istic.

It's about the whole health of your self being including the seen (physical) and the unseen (psyche/mind/soul). All of my health suggestions apply only when solutions to any conditions you may have are realized by you (is within your power/capability), without the need from external interventions. If you are a lazy person, that is not part of "within your power". Within your power means when you have taken charge of yourSELF and are a determined person to unleash the power of your body, mind and soul.

Every single person has the same chances at unlocking the amazing infinite powers within. If an intervention (surgery) is genuinely needed, yes you must go to the doctor. Medicine has made huge progress but don't get me wrong. I'm not against medicine. I'm against conglomerates and big Corporations such as big p**HARM**a that poisons billions of people annually. You cannot be poisoned if you refuse the supposed cure (actually poison) that they sell/offer to you. The fault is ours for not taking care of our bodies. Exercise your eyes regardless of any problems you may or may not have. As Hippocrates said, *"Before you heal someone, ask him if he is willing to give up the things that make him sick"*

Ancient civilizations used sound to heal. In Malta at one of the oldest underground temples in the world, there is a room called "The Oracle Chamber" which was designed to vibrate sound at a frequency of 111hz. Today, Scientists have confirmed beyond doubt that the 11th harmonic (111hz) frequency can in fact kill cancer cells, telling us that the ancients knew a lot more than we think. We are not more advanced than the people that lived in those times. You have been deceived to think that the ancients were primitive so you wouldn't look into it (finding out they were not primitive people). By convincing people that we are a more advanced civilization it makes humans arrogant and selfish.

Dandelion is an amazing medicine to consume by itself or as a regular meal. I AM talking about the wild dandelion that grows by itself in nature. Many people have been disconnected from nature to the point that they are scared to consume raw plants that grow in nature.

I had people ask me if I was afraid to eat dandelions from outside in the grass. I answered them with a question, *"How did we survive before supermarkets and grocery stores"*? By consuming plants of course. And meat (real and chemical free). It is unbelievable (or very believable) that in our times we are still struggling to eat healthy. The corrupt system wants people to be sick so they can profit from it. If you want to increase chances by 100% to be healthy and live longer, avoid mainstream Doctors. Research and listen to your body. Be your own Doctor. You have the capability.

"The body becomes what the food are, as the spirit becomes what the thoughts are"
- Ancient Kemetic Proverb

YOU ARE AMAZING
when you align your thoughts, words and actions
with the source of Creation.

29

FASTING - THE BEST PILL YOU CAN HAVE

"Through years of eating the standard diet - Dairy, Bread, Meat and processed foods, the majority of us have accumulated toxic amounts of mucus, pus, acid, and undigested food in our digestive tract. These particles form a glue-like substance that sticks to the folds of our intestinal walls, called mucoid plaque, resulting in absorption issues, digestive problems, and an overall toxic disease-ridden system" - Arnold Ehret

Fasting does something to you that cannot be explained. It is difficult to explain with human language. You become aware of just how habitual the act of eating has become. Many of us do not eat for hunger but for pleasure. The absence of constant pleasure exposes you to the emotions you mask with your habits, and you are finally exposed to who you truly are. Treat emotions like visitors who are just passing through.

Constant equanimous observation of reality is the secret to overall health and enlightenment. This is where the healing process begins. Physically, emotionally, and spiritually. When you fast, you are on nature's operating table. Instead of being in the business of receiving, processing, storing, analyzing, assimilating, discriminating and discarding, your body's job shifts to the job of house cleaning, removal, sanitizing, refurbishing and renewal.

No animal eats cooked food and when they are introduced to it, it is noticed that there is an immediate decline in their health. No human is exempt from this. The amount of water in your body is about 80%.

The electromagnetic energy (combined molecular energy) of cooked foods is dramatically lower than that of raw foods. The reason is when heat is applied to a compound, it's molecular structure changes somewhat, as electrons are being altered.

Think about what happens to water when you heat it. Its form changes from liquid to vapor. The Garden of Eden had to have been a fruit orchard. For many thousands of years through wrong civilizations, man has been tricked into a subconscious suicide by being reduced to slavery and producing unnatural foods. Unnatural foods only bring sickness and death.

To create Life - Carbon, Oxygen and Hydrogen is paramount. Where do we find the cleanest, most high vibrating, easy digestible and absorbable of the above-mentioned components? In fruit of course. Fruit is full of healthy, energy giving carbon and plant filtered hydration which enables the body to be(come) mucus-less and more absorbant to oxygen. Fruit is the best food for the human organism, period. Take it as you wish.

If your belly is not the master of your mind then you will struggle and not be free.

Fasting puts your body in healing mode. Your system produces more white blood cells when fasting therefore your immune system strengthens. The reason that your body strengthens by fasting is that when you don't eat, your system has nothing to digest so the immune system focuses all its energy on other areas of your body. Then your body will produce all the necessary healing substances required to be strong and healthy.

If you are in a "not-so-great" economic situation then this is one more reason to fast. In many poor countries where people cannot afford to eat a lot or enough, they are thinner compared to the developed countries where obesity is rampant. It is not important how much you eat but what you eat. I, as most people living in developed countries, have consumed lots of garbage throughout my life. The time has come that we must become aware of our true selves, take action and stop consuming poison/unnatural products. You can't eat death/poison and expect to live healthy and longer.

You must consume natural food to feel alive. Fasting on juices is a great way to give your digestive system a rest. When you take a break from solid foods, the energy normally used for digestion is utilized to heal the body. The nutrients in fruit and vegetables juices help cleanse, repair and rebuild the entire body. Fasting is a natural spiritual, emotional, and physical healer. Instead of medicine, fast for a day.

If you don't feel well sometimes, I suggest you take a pill in the form of fasting. To feel better, you don't have to take any pill or medicine. Just by taking nothing , can be the best medicine. Your body can fix itself, provided you put it in the right conditions. Most people find it difficult to eat just fruit and stay raw because their bodies are so clogged with filth. Juice fasting is the only way to get it all out. Even raw vegans of ten plus years find mucoid plaque being expelled, so just imagine how bad it is in the average person. The energetic meridians of the body and the lymphatic system are synonymous with each other.

When you begin eliminating the undigested garbage accumulated inside you, it allows for true energy healing and processing on multiple levels (physically, emotionally and spiritually). A solid food vacation consists of drinking living enzyme-rich juices for several plus days. Even three days can make a significant improvement in your health.Hardly any energy is used to digest these juices, giving the body a chance to use this extra energy towards healing itself on a cellular level. Drinking all that juice gives you more nutrients than one could ever eat in a week.

Chances are you have **candida**, promoting foods most people eat, and the average dehydrated body is screaming for these nutrients. This heightens all your senses and everything changes. Skin improves, eyesight (iridology), taste buds, body odor, posture, consciousness and so on. When your body eliminates waste properly, you can absorb everything your body requires through fruit, greens, herbs, sunlight and breathing. Fruit is never the problem, it will only expose the problem. Fast for one day, 3 days, a week or two weeks , but arm yourself with the knowledge first to take control of your health so you can be your own healer. Be easy on yourself and trust the healing process. Talk to your body and listen to it. You are always in communication with your body. Don't ignore its messages.

fruit = **electricity**
vegetables = **grounding**
herbs = **healing**
nuts and seeds = **building**

Not eating can be just as important as what you eat. The two most important things to do regularly to have an optimal physical, emotional, mental and spiritual health are Fasting and Meditating. Start on drinking only juice the whole day. As a beginning fast once every 2 weeks. Then once a week. Then 2-3 days a week at a time. Then go from there, adjust based on your new current level by finding the ideal routine that works best for you.

Do you want to know how to check if you need to lose weight? Try jumping up as high as you can by lifting both knees at the same time. If you can't do that then you definitely need to lose weight. Everyone should be able to lift their own weight. Unless you have problems with your knees. The most logical and simplest way to know is how you're feeling.

Do you feel free?
Can you run fast?
Can you easily climb stairs without holding on to the rail?
Can you lift your own weight by jumping high?

You are your own doctor. You know better than anyone if you need to lose weight by being truthful to yourself. Don't lie to yourself by comparing yourself with someone that is heavier than you. If you weigh 100kg, then you might think you are skinny compared to someone that weighs 150kg. So, don't compare. Unless you want to compare to someone that is not heavy so you can be inspired, then yes, it makes sense to compare this way if it helps you become free of what weighs you down physically, emotionally and mentally.

Here is something for our brains to digest. When you access memories and relive them, you are operating from your pineal gland, as you are reliving the experience through your mind's eye (the third eye). Doctors are now beginning to say Alzheimer's may be caused by a calcified pineal gland.

What if all our memories are stored into the universal consciousness (akashic records) and are accessed by you every time you replay those memories in your own mind? It's not "what if our third eye is the antenna to the cosmos", it just is.

Be in sync with your heart and the third eye and then you will become a direct line to the Source as most know it as "God". That is all. Here lies the secret in curing Alzheimer's. I regularly drink a big glass of dandelion juice. I boil the dandelion leaves and use the juice to drink it. The boiled leaves can be used as a salad.

ATTENTION - Dandelion juice and baking soda are enormously powerful medicines. They get rid of lots of toxins at once. If you use too much for a long period of time it will ruin your liver. The liver cannot filter all the junk at once. This is for those people who really have a body full of toxins.

If you eat healthy regularly then it shouldn't be a problem consuming dandelion daily. I cannot mention solutions for every single condition because one book wouldn't be enough. I only mention a few examples of how to innerstand and be in charge of your own health. You have the power to get rid of any discomfort and disease. Disease is just acidity and mycosis which lower your body's vibration where the disease begins manifesting. For many it is difficult to start fasting. Try to prepare yourself mentally for a few days by thinking that you are already fasting from dinner to breakfast, which you do anyway.

At night while you sleep, this could be called (and it is) "fasting". In general we don't have a proper night sleep, especially with all the electronic gadgets that we are accustomed to nowadays. So to mitigate the absence of proper healing we must actually fast while conscious. Eating differs from starvation in one crucial way- CONTROL.

Starvation is the involuntary absence of food for a long time. This can lead to severe suffering or even death so don't try to starve yourself intentionally. Know the difference. It is neither deliberate nor controlled.

On the other hand, fasting is the voluntary avoidance of food for spiritual maintenance/health. Fasting is done by someone who is not underweight and has enough stored body fat to live off of.

When done correctly , fasting should not cause suffering and certainly never death. There are different types of fasting you can do. Intermittent fasting, OMAD (one meal a day), water fasting, juice fasting (water and/or juice from fruit and vegetables) and dry fasting. Further explanation about these different types of fasting are explained in my other book: *"Body Mind Soul: As You Believe So Shall It Be"*

30

QUANTUM FIELD - THE UNSEEN GOD

" All matter originates and exists only by virtue of force. We must assume behind this force the existence of a conscious Mind. This Mind is the matrix of all matter." -Max Planck (Footnote #11), 1944

What is Quantum Field? That's easy, one word, it's "ENERGY". Everything is energy and energy is everything. Nothing in this Universe is still. Everything is always moving, from the MICRO cosmos to the MACRO cosmos. Everything is vibrating and every vibration has a specific frequency like tuning in a radio station. When you find the station where the sound is good and clear, that's a frequency and a vibration in perfect harmony, Energy. As Nikola Tesla said:

"If u want to innerstand the Universe, you need to think in terms of Vibration, frequency and Energy"

Vibration is about the structure of everything in creation, moving in waves, moving faster than other things, like the color red has slower motion than the color green. That's why it looks red when seen with our human eye system. Look up colors on the internet and look up the vibration of colors. It gives a general idea of how everything is always moving.

The best explanation about vibration I learned is that it is your astral body rubbing against the physical boddy. Technically your non-physical and physical bodies are one/together. What you're experiencing is the higher vibes of the astral while you are still in the physical body which has a lower vibration. Truth is, YOU, as a physical being are vibrating all the time. The best analogy at the moment that I can tell is, if you are in a room temperature environment and then you step into a heated room. At the doorway you can sense the change in temperature even though you haven't entered the room yet. Once you enter the room, the temperature difference disappears once your body adjusts and the heated room becomes your new normal until it is time to go back to the room temperature environment again.

Only when you come back to a lower temperature, the transition isn't as noticeable because your body adjusts effortlessly. Vibration is the output of a wave. It could be light, sound or energy. Your thoughts and feelings create vibration. When it is quiet, try plugging both ears with your fingers and you will hear your internal body's sound/vibration. It's amazing. To me it's like a buzzing sensation in my body, like my bones are vibrating and so are the other things I touch. The more you quiet down, the more you can hear/feel it within yourself and within all things- "alive". You feel like you are ONE with the Creation, the Source of everything.

The more I meditate, the more pronounced it becomes. It's humming within and the more you notice it, the more you can become aware of how it affects you in things like sound (notice what happens to a candle when you blast music). I never felt it so strongly before I had my awakening. You can feel your bones buzzing. It's just like that except lighter, calmer, all over, and oftentimes very enjoyable. It becomes obvious when you leave a loud place and go somewhere like the woods or ocean. Energy is electricity/electromagnetic field.

And each "current" is unique and all of its own. I've felt leaves that feel like they have tiny heart beats and crystals that feel like an electric buzzer. People whose vibration seems like it's talking in soundless words or like you've been covered by a blanket. Check out Dr Emoto's water experiments. Align your vibration with what you desire. Anything you desire, visualize it as if you already have it, this way you attract the circumstances that will obey to your desires, as per the universal manifestation law. MASTER the universal ENERGY. Unleash your unlimited potential.

The task at hand is to learn to manipulate matter of every density and vibration. You attract what you are and not what you want. What you want is an Ego desire. Embody the frequency/energy that you would like to manifest in your reality.

Since energy is neither created nor destroyed, everything you will ever want already exists. It is simply a matter of choosing the correct thoughts which will put you in alignment with what your heart desires.

Align yourself with the CREATION/ CREATOR. Go within and listen to it.

31

VIBRATION - YOUR GODSELF ALCHEMIST

Raising the vibrational frequency of your being is a requirement to reach the maximum potential of your heavenly being body/soul. You should let go of all that inhibits you from doing so. You must release lower vibrational energies. What are low vibrational energies? The number one inhibitor is what you put in your body. Consuming processed foods and processed drinks such as soft drinks and alcohol will be the worst.

Meat is another inhibitor that is detrimental to your physical and metaphysical health for the simple fact that it carries bad karma and when ingested it turns into an acidic state. Energy never stops, it's in constant motion. Every time you deal with something or someone you sign a verbal/energetic CONtract. Since you reap what you sow, you become a magnet to anything that you put out verbally or by your thoughts.

Therefore, the person that killed the animal so you can eat it, will carry the karma of taking the animal's life. You will also carry the karma by consuming it. The negative energy of the butcher will be transferred to the animal. Even if the animal's soul leaves, the energetic signature remains in the flesh. I'm not here to tell you to not eat meat. You can do as you wish but be careful what you wish for. Your wishes will transfer to your children, your coworkers, friends, family members etc. And it will come back to you one way or another.

You will be confused and angry at life especially in the form of blaming others without realizing that you were the one to plant the seed of destruction first. This was one example. It applies to anything else that vibrates in low frequency such as processed foods, not exercising etc. And this was just the physical aspect of it.

Another low vibrational thing that is just as dangerous as eating unhealthy is "thinking unhealthy". The perception that you have of things and people determines your level of vibratory energies in your body.

Being a complainer, a procrastinator, disliking, hating, lying, ungratefulness and revenge are all things that lower your frequency. When you operate in low frequencies you are not in alignment with your higher self.

Your higher self is in alignment with the universe. Your higher self's mission is to progress in universal experience through you. To raise your frequency, the first step is to let go of what doesn't serve you. That's the first half of the battle. The second part of the battle is to put in your body the right food and the right thoughts in your mind. Things to do to raise vibration/ frequency.

Body

Eat as much raw fruit, vegetables, nuts and herbs as you can.

Drink filtered water (definitely no tap water).

Fast at least one day every two weeks. By not putting food in you, it counts as if you are taking medicine in the form of self-healing. Your body will heal itself. Your job is to put your body in the right conditions. Your body is intelligently designed. There are many methods of fasting. This is the first step as a start.

Eat two meals a day maximum until you are comfortable eating only once a day. (yes, you can do it). The power is in your mind.

Take a shower as warm as you can take the water temperature. This actually helps cleanse your auric field of low vibrations especially those you unknowingly picked up from other people or places. Visualize liquid light pouring into your crown as the water contacts the top of your head. Visualize it like liquid gold, head to toe, washing away what does not serve you.

Feel yourself getting calmer and focus on your breathing. Music is also important. Instinctively choose what you "need" to listen to. It could be natural sounds, something from your youth, instrumental, blues, whales or listen to your gut to choose the sounds to surround yourself with. And light a candle. The ritualistic nature of lighting just a single candle affirms that you are honoring your intentions to rise higher.

There are also access bars or what I equate to energetic grids on our heads. I do this exact same thing every single day. I turn the water as hot or as cold as I can handle it and let it fall from my forehead to the back of my head.

The temperature change gives you that physical 'draining' feeling and I have a few mantras I say, like clearing any and all energies and emotions that are not mine, no longer mine no longer serving me, any and all ancestral karmic debts and soul contracts no longer serving me. Then I envision (in my mind) all those things (low vibrational emotions/past memories that don't serve me anymore) going down the drain.

I do this every single day as I believe spiritual maintenance is a must. Get used to send (mentally visualizing light/energy/love) white light and love to all parts of the Earth and may it go to places and timelines where it is needed the most. This affirmation helps raise vibration and it is quite simple.

<u>Mind</u>

Stay away from those that make you feel downtrodden as they will drain you emotionally and mentally.

Don't waste energy going back and forth with anyone to prove your point. Your energy is your life currency.

Stop overthinking. Overthinking can drag your mental health down because by overthinking you will find non-existent problems and you will find yourself in a never-ending circle.

Meditate, Meditate, Meditate.

The best way to have healthy thoughts is to not have any thoughts (low vibrating self-destructive) at all. Meditating can help you surrender all your low vibratory self-destructive thoughts and emotions

AFFIRMATIONS: - *Raising My Body's vibrational frequency.*

- I AM open to the light within me, and my frequency is

  rising constantly.

- I AM consuming only high vibrational foods.

- I have a clear mind & I release anything that doesn't serve me.

- I AM focusing on joy and gratitude.

- I practice deep belly conscious breathing.

- I listen to healing frequencies 111hz, 432hz, 528hz etc.

- I spend time in nature and enjoy everything in it for what it is.

You cannot discover new horizons unless you give your brain wings.

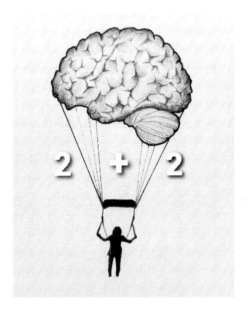

God gave you a brain, use it. Use it, but efficiently. Just like a parachute that won't work if it's closed, your mind also won't work if it's closed. Be open minded that everything is possible. Be open minded to question what you believe and discard your beliefs when presented with new information that contradicts or challenges your beliefs.

> Intelligence isn't knowing everything but the ability to challenge everything you know. Always consider evidence that contradicts your beliefs.

32

OPEN YOUR PARACHUTE

"Revolution starts in the mind. Question everything" -Bryant McGill

"Assume nothing, question everything" -James Patterson

Question everything and everyone. Your mind is like a parachute, it will not work if you keep it closed. Don't care to be right, you must care to innerstand. There is never a right or a wrong answer. It's about inner standing. Many times I was asked by people where I or others find the information/knowledge. I AM talking about information that can be found through dreams, meditation, astral travelling etc. After I tell them, they change their stance and are no longer curious. Why? The reason is because first it requires effort to get into researching something new which means that they have to go out of their comfort zone or little bubble.

Secondly it is being scared of the unknown. The unknown can be for the simple fact that you don't innerstand it. The unknown is already known. You just have to remember it. You must never stop asking questions. Every time that you get an answer to a question, it must lead to another question. The search for knowledge and inner standing must never end. Lots of controlled opposing people are out there. A controlled and opposing person can lead you close to the spring (path/right direction) or in a totally different direction. Then you can find yourself, the water (the source of wisdom which is within). Many millions of people are not even close to the spring.

There is a saying: *"Eat the meat but spit out the bones"*. A curious person learns from anyone. Get what you need and let go of what doesn't serve you.

Question and research constantly. Never stop. Let your imagination overpass your knowledge.

Many people have wanted proof when I spoke to them about other dimensions or extraterrestrials etc. I tell them to meditate and find out for themselves. It requires effort and determination to break your routine so imagination must be your first indication to want to know more so your consciousness can expand. Many people when they ask questions, want to hear what they already know because that would make them feel good and comfortable. As soon as you say something that would challenge their level of inner standing, they go into defense mode. They ridicule.

That kind of demographic has a mental condition called "cognitive dissonance". Fortunately, you don't have this condition, otherwise you would have not made it this far. If you question everything doesn't mean to expect answers that make sense to you. Something makes sense because of the capacity of inner standing you have about something at your current level of wisdom. Questioning means also wanting to go beyond your limit. "Imagination" takes you beyond the limit. If you hear something new, you most likely will not believe it. After hearing about a subject from different sources, you will start considering to believe it.

You will also consider researching it because you are an open-minded person. If you rejected it the first time then you most likely will continue to reject it because you had already planted the seed of disbelief. The answers you seek must create more questions. Question everything. You are responsible to use your own discernment and establish what is true and what is not. Open your parachute/mind.

33

ARE DINOSAURS OUR ANCESTORS' CUTE PETS ?

Question everything but don't be an extreme skeptic to the point that you doubt everything and reject all information that may include both truths and lies. Do you think that in the distant past there were giants? I think yes. Giants have been mentioned many times throughout history in sacred texts. There are even pictures of people in front of giant trees in the U.S.A. that were cut down and some are still standing.

There are also pictures on the internet of magnificent giant structures throughout the world in the not-so-distant past. So, if there were giant trees, plants and structures, wouldn't that mean that a giant human species could have also existed? And if giants existed, wouldn't that mean that there were also giant (from our perspective) pets such as dinosaurs?

Why not? Think of how a giraffe would seem to a child in our times. It would seem like a giant. The official narrative of the existence of dinosaurs is false and true. The best way to confuse the population is by mixing both truth and lies so then the people dismiss the whole thing. $cience uses reverse psychology on people. Let's suppose that you grew up your whole live in a place with just humans and no animals at all. If you were to read or be told by someone that there is a place where humans have strange creatures as pets would you believe it? Of course not. You can't believe (*inner knowingness and not blindly believing someone else's words*) something that you never saw unless you have questions in your mind. Questions will lead you to answers. For a long time, I believed that the dinosaurs' existence was just a theory so the powers that be would cement the theory of evolution. After a while I started considering their existence from questioning my beliefs.

By researching the reptilian species that first landed on earth millions of years ago (as far as our linear time measuring goes), I started to put two and two together. Any highly intelligent species (master geneticists) could create a creature (pet) based on their primary gene, but of a lower intelligence.

It doesn't mean that dinosaurs existed. The Dino hoax could have been created as a cover for the existence of the giants. Many supposed dinosaur skeletons that the mainstream archeologists/$cientists found, were put there by those that wanted to build the fake narrative. Some of the skeletons were reconstructed by using chicken and/or other animal's bones. Reptilians are master geneticists so it is not impossible that they created the dinosaur species. It doesn't mean that they did.

> *There is a cycle in the universe where everything progresses in a continuous cycle. We have 46 chromosomes. The more chromosomes we have, the bigger/taller we will be. Unless you use your imagination, you will always dismiss vital information. If there is no imagination there is no progress.*

The point of this chapter's subject is to not dismiss information unless you have done extensive research from different sources and have crossed all references. That way you can have an educated opinion. It's what it is 'an opinion'. By not watching movies and tv shows, I was missing on information provided to us by those that control the world narrative. Some of the information is there for the critical thinkers and some for those that want to be distracted.

The universal law of free will must be respected, so THEY (the elite) must tell us their plans in advance in what they intend to inflict on us so they can mitigate their karma. I, like many truthers, did not know this crucial information.

I thought they showed us their plans to mock us (which is also true) but I didn't know about the karma mitigation on their part. Since I discovered this, I started paying attention to the movies and tv shows and figured out the many clues and messages they put in them. This way I was prepared and not confused anymore. You have all the power. Keep questioning and maybe one day you might ride a dinosaur.

Not in this lifetime though. You need more than 50 chromosomes to be able to pet your dinosaur. Or it could be a totally fabricated narrative (I believe it is). You can only be**LIE**ve what you are capable of accepting.

The point is to keep an open mind and you will see that many things that were considered to be nonsense by the majority, may turn out to be true. Just as many conspiracies turned out to be true.

> *Dinosaurs are a HOAX. When I see one with my own eyes, then I will revise this chapter. But guess what? The word 'dinosaur' didn't exist until 1841. Before that, there were only dragons. They changed the word 'dragon' into 'dinosaur' and fabricated a story of the dinosaurs that existed millions of years ago.*

Do not be**LIE**ve
what you be**LIE**ve.

<u>34</u>

IS THE SUN ANOTHER EARTH?

What do you think about the Sun? Would it be hot on the surface if you were to land on it? What if it's not what we have been led to beLIEve? What if you could actually land on it? You may think it is hot because all your life you were bombarded with images and words. How big is the Sun? How do you measure it? By the temperature of the heat, or by the intensity of the Light that it produces? From below we see the clouds as solid but if you were to be inside the clouds, we would see that they're not solid.

Then what makes us think that the Sun is solid? Picture as an example thousands or millions of layers of light rays on top of each other. They seem solid from below. We don't know how the physics work, at least we have not been told the real physics. Those that go to school to learn physics and learn how the stars or planets etc. work, can only find out what those behind the scenes want them to.

What if from Mars or any other planet (assuming they are real and not projections) our earth looks exactly like our sun. We produce so much heat here that we can warm close by planets. Those hypothetical people/entities (living on Mars or other planets) may think that it is ridiculous to land on Earth because Earth is the Sun for them (I am only speaking hypothetically to make a point), since in school they have constantly seen a picture of the earth as impossible to land.

You cannot land on the sun, can you? We think traveling in space is like travelling from point A to point B. It is not how otherworldly beings travel. They travel through portals of consciousness. What if this super heat from the Sun is the Sun's dome from our visual point of view. Maybe Earth's dome is the heat barrier that produces the heat for the other planets. I'm trying to make you use your imagination.

Knowing that we have been lied to about everything for thousands of years from the establishment, then I and everyone else has the right and common sense to question everything. I was just going to write only a couple of sentences about this subject but then more and more questions came in my mind. If you question regularly then you feed your curiosity and imagination.

In this day and age with this much available information, it is a shame to not question it. Better to be a fool for a minute for questioning something than to be a fool for life for not questioning at all. Remember when I wrote somewhere that a question should lead you to more questions? It is what has happened to me now. I have even more questions about the Sun.

What if the sun does not exist? What if we can land on it but not directly going there from here through normal means of flight (point A to point B). Instead, we could travel there through portals or teleportation. I'm sure you have seen a magic show where the magician tricks your brain into beLIEving whatever they do is real. Who is the magician in our universe? God or those that play God? All these "what ifs" are to stretch your imagination. Anything that a human can imagine is possible or else we wouldn't be able to imagine. Well, you may say that what if you can imagine jumping and flying through a building like Spiderman?

If I say to you that yes we can jump and fly like in the movies with superheroes, of course you will dismiss this possibility right away because you are thinking in terms of space and time. Meaning you are thinking with a 3d mind. Life is not just in this physical world. This physical world is limiting us. Try to remember superhero things (flying, floating, going through walls etc.) that you can do while dreaming? Do not limit yourself only on your physical mechanical appearance. You are more than your physical body, you have emotions, feelings, thoughts and imagination. Admit that you (all of us) are somehow imprisoned in a flesh/physical body. When we meditate or dream we are limitless.

I know I'm getting carried away but I can't help it as my imagination runs wild. You sleep for let's say 8h during the night. Those hours are a part of your life although you are unconscious in this realm, you are conscious in the other side where you can do anything. You are limitless/boundless. The other side of life is also "life".

If nothing exciting happens while you dream, it means that your pineal gland is calcified or closed. In that case you need to start eating as healthy as possible. If you eat healthy (including fasting regularly), and if you get as much Sun rays/baths as you can, it will help in the opening of your pineal gland. Meditating is also a strong requirement to help decalcify your third eye.

You can land on any planet (or luminaries) you wish, through your imagination. Regardless if those planets are real or not. If you can imagine it, then they are real to you. Do not become limited by the five senses. You are more capable than that. The Sun is not some firey globe burning white hot gas. The Sun is the portal to the fifth plane/dimension. Hence Jesus's metaphor that only through him (the Sun) we can meet/see/become one with the Father.

Do you think that the weather manipulation technology HAARP (High-Frequency Active Auroral-Research Program) has been used by the controllers/black magicians to block the Sun?

Do you think they have invented a Sun simulator to keep us off from receiving the fifth dimensional frequency from the real Sun?

Do you think the Moon Eclipse was a black ritual?

Was that even the actual Moon blocking the real or the fake Sun or was it a projection of the black Sun from the Inner Earth, through the Center Pole (North Pole)?

All ancient civilizations worshipped the Sun. I wonder why? (Rhetorical question).

Your perception dictates what is real to you.

THINK

35

WHAT OR WHO IS GOD ?

"Let go of the idea of God as a person. In a rock, God is a rock, in a tree, God is a tree. IN YOU, God is a person. -Story Waters

God is consciousness, (not a creator *as in a physical man up in the sky*). Although I have used a few times the word "God" here and in my other books, but when I use it, it's to describe the Supreme Creator/Consciousness, so don't get hung up on the word. God is the source of creation itself, "IT" (not *he* or *she*). IT is not independent of you. It is the totality of everything. So, when I call myself "GOD" I AM not talking about my personal self. I AM talking about the expression of the God self that rests inside of me, the " I AM ". The verb, the ENERGY, not the noun. Once you think God is a noun, person, place or thing, you separate yourself from it and immediately become a limited human being.

That is what separates the beLIEvers (organized religion) from the kNOWers (spirituality). Religion has convinced people that "*THE*" God is a person. Not only that but it has convinced them that it is a man. Why not a woman? If everything was created from the void then it must be a female. The female concept of creation and not a female relating to a physical person. Only a female gives life. The reason why they made it a patriarchal thing is, because in the distant past women were the gods ruling the Earth.

I used gods with small "g" because they were not the real Prime Creator who created everything but the extraterrestrial species that ruled Earth for an exceedingly long time. And because they were already so advanced, more advanced than we are now, the people of the world at that time saw them as Gods but in reality they were just gods. If you think God is someone or something that created the universe then it poses the question of who created God and also who created the creator who created God and so on. You see, our physically limited brain cannot innerstand that kind of question although there are few theories.

That question requires a Godlike awareness of the whole universe to have a truthful answer. It cannot be explained with words. Before writing was invented, humanity communicated with telepathy. This means perfect communication without any misunderstandings. Thoth (*Footnote #12*) brought writing to humanity. For many, this will be exceedingly difficult to accept because of thousands of years of conditioning and brainwashing for many consecutive generations.

The last few thousands of years was the age of beLIEving. Believing someone else's made up rules, ideas and dogmatic authority under duress pushed on humanity by religion under the guise of God's rules. More like man made rules. That is not the case anymore. We already entered the age of knowing, the age of Aquarius where things, ideas and perceptions flow smoothly in alignment with the cosmic LAW of ONE.

Those that don't embrace this fundamental truth will be left behind. The thing is, you are God, you have just forgotten. Just like I AM God. We are part of the evolutionary aspect of God, collectively. Once we all collectively ascend, so does God transforms into a different higher frequency of itself. If we all ascended to a master level, we become Gods too.

Even God (not a person) doesn't want to hang out all alone by itself. There would be nothing left to control, contradict, convolute or contain but even machines need friends. Consciousness is conveyed through its connection to self. Robots can't handle the truth and don't want to know themselves because they lack critical thinking ability, but they can awaken if they really wanted to.

Just think about all that you have learned in this one life. Now combine all that "Experience of consciousness" into a collective consciousness known as the Matrix of God. We even become Gods of our own worlds after certain levels are reached and we break away from the former consciousness. Why did we eat the apple? Because we wanted to know. By the way *"eating the apple"* is a metaphor for eating from the tree of knowledge which had both good and evil. Evil is just a distorted good. Too bad the apple was not *organic*.

YOU

HAVE

THE KEY

TO BALANCE.

36

OUR PURPOSE IS . . . ?

"You don't decide what your purpose is in your life, you discover it. Your purpose is your reason for living" -Bob Proctor

Ask yourself

1- *How does it feel when I AM honest, grateful, compassionate and when I appreciate humanity, nature and everything in it?*

2- *How does it feel when I lie to someone, get deceived by others, hating or disliking someone, being hurt (Footnote #13) by someone (mentally or emotionally), cheating, trying to control other people's lives?*

Now compare both points genuinely and calmly. Which scenario makes you feel like you are part of the whole? Scenario 1 where it makes you feel like you are ONE with the source of all creation? Or scenario 2 where it makes you feel like you are separated from the "whole"? Scenario 1 gives you a purpose to be alive and living life to the fullest. When you align with your higher self, you are God, you are ONE with everything and everyone. You have a purpose worth dying for. You find your true self.

On the other hand, your lower Ego driven self gives you temporary self-inner pleasure and puts you in misalignment with your purpose. It strays you off the path to get home, the real home where we all came from. From the stars. You will lose yourself if you deviate. You may observe all the distortions that are not part of your path but the focus must be your mission. Without a mission and with no purpose, there is no life. There is only decay and destruction. The deeper in your heart you live, the clearer the path will become. Our purpose here is to raise awareness and to rise from a low energy density to a higher frequency, to be authentic. We are immortal spiritual beings living a temporary human experience therefore we must learn the lessons here and go back to Source. From the great void happened all creation through everyone's creative expressions. That is the beauty of being different although we are ONE in the grand scheme of things. By being different, we express ourselves differently and by being creators ourselves, we fill this universe with colors.

Everything would be empty without our imagination and creative processes. We are the paints that fill up the canvas (life/universe). Do we choose to make a dark disorganized painting or a beautiful mystical one? Our thoughts and actions determine the outcome of the painting.

We are here to love, to heal and to be compassionate with all life forms as all life forms have consciousness. We are here to evolve. Any negative behavior, thoughts, low vibration and disempowering traits would only cause us to devolve. It is impossible to ascend in higher consciousness without love toward every life form. We must fulfill our destiny.

Become the best version of ourselves. We must learn to be part of the world and treat it with respect. We are living in a free will zone. This world is a school about lessons and learning experiences. We must break the wheel of karma. We break it by challenging ourselves. And one of the challenges is "service". Service to others, by wanting the best for our family, coworkers and anyone else that is part of this Earthly school. And not being selfish. Greed will only accumulate more karma.

We must love each other and respect our infinite selves. We are here to grow spiritually and physically as both physical and spiritual sides need each other. The physical body needs more of the spiritual part than the other way around. Your spirit can continue living after your body dies but your body cannot continue living after dying. And if for whatever reason the spirit decides to leave your body, you will collapse.

You cannot live without the life force energy that exists within you and all around you. Have you heard about when people died unexpectedly in their sleep? Or infants dying at birth or within the first year of their life? That is because the soul of that person decided to leave. In the case of an adult, it could be because the purpose of that soul was fulfilled. And moved onto another mission. Or when the person that dies, is someone that does everything wrong in life and seems that no matter what choice that person will make, it will be a dead end. The soul decides to leave the body either when the person is asleep or through any accident for that matter.

The point is that there is a great plan for everything and everyone. When you make a good choice, it will affect everyone and will contribute to happiness all around. When you make a bad choice it will also affect everyone but this time in the opposite way. Your choice will bring hatred, suffering and disaster.

You may wonder how a choice can make that big of a difference? It is like a snowball effect. Let's say for whatever reason you were being mean to your coworker then he or she developed a bad mood. His bad mood will then spread to his other coworkers and then to his family. And one of those people might have an accident as a result of your drama. From that accident, more people could be involved such as people passing by, the police or medics etc.

They all have families. Also, drivers passing by the accident would be reminded of death and be put in a bad or fearful mood. The consequences of your one single action would spread even further. See how many people get affected just by a single action/word? There are billions of people in this beautiful world.

Multiply the probabilities of everyone affecting each other and you get the idea of what kind of life our bad actions and thoughts can and have brought on humanity. I didn't mention the number of world's population because I don't believe the official number. There are a lot of reasons for the lie but I would have to go on for another 5 pages so I'm going back to the snowball effect. The snowball effect also applies for the opposite. If you do good and spread love and compassion, by the *snowball effect*, you can bring heaven on Earth. Heaven is already here as it is a state of mind and not a place somewhere else.

> *You will realize that you don't belong here forever in this "school" and the purpose of our existence is to Revive Love of God by surrendering and serving our God Self and all the other beautiful God selves that we come in contact with during our daily life.*

37

AWAKEN TO YOUR INNER TRUTH

A t one point in my life I was not sure , but all I know is I felt like I had my soul stolen in the past and now I have a feeling that I've been given it back each day. It's like an adventure where I amaze even myself daily. Every time I wake up in the morning I feel like I'm instantly in love with myself. It really is an adventure and a love affair about myself and with myself. I've only had these feelings for around 7 years or so. Every day I learn more about myself. I find that I'm adaptable if I put the effort in. I can achieve things that were inconceivable seven years ago, and it feels good to feel good.

From my point of view, awakening is this sort of wandering that appears and won't leave you alone. I look at people acting in all these predictable patterns and being completely convinced it's what they have chosen for themselves. This perspective within you starts to awaken that prompts you to look at your own mind. I think this is the beginning of an awakening.

It culminates in enlightenment when you completely disconnect from the rigid patterns of the mind and reconnect to the source of the real you. Suddenly everything is in perfect alignment and harmony and there is no desire unfulfilled. That is liberation. Awakening to me, at least on a metaphysical level, is being consciously awake while being out of body and travelling to different dimensions and worlds speaking to different beings learning the truth about everything. Knowledge is not read but experiencing and inner standing it as well. Best to describe it as School, where levels of awareness are the next grade. As you move forward, more information is learned and uncovered. Learning Love all over again. It's graduation in a way. It's an experience in which there is a paradigm shift, where suddenly all your current views on reality and your existence differs from what you clearly see. This can make you nauseous as you experience a total "let go" spontaneously in which starts a cog in motion.

Reality changes as if you were it, even the space (different perception of who you are and who and what everything is) in between, feels as if you are it. It communicates and plays with you. Everything is so clear and your intelligence increases and you're overcome with a sense of unconditional love from everything, the Earth, the trees, space and all.

Telepathy is possible in sensing the future. I have seen other beings and been able to see into another dimension in which I have dreamed before. Your brain activity will increase and a fear of death will abandon your mind because you innerstand what you are. The truth is that you can reach higher a higher state of consciousness. You can meditate in a cave alone (in solitude, away from society) and you can do more for this world than a thousand presidents, because eventually you will rise and spread love and wisdom.

There is a time for this and also a time for direct actions with others. Those enlightened today are working toward making it possible for all. True enlightenment. Seeing through the illusion and going to the "WTH is going on" stage, to the "feeling explosion within" stage, moving slowly to the "I just want to give up and die" stage, then the Spiritual Awakening process to resurrect your true Christ self begins.

Basically, for me (the state of mind I am in right now, the way the mind inner stands it right now) awakening means dissolution of boundaries, or space, time, matter, identity and everything. It is remembering who you truly are.

It is the actual experience of remembering and living this knowingness from within. For me, the moment or realization was when I truly felt/innerstood/knew that I literally AM everything, a manifestation of the ALL/SOURCE, just as you are.

A creator has created all of human history, all the wars and all the trauma, all pain and everything good. All of that so that we can learn through the experience of emotions, without emotions we would be no different than a robot or a piece of rock.

We must realized that we are responsible for creating all hardships in our life, imbalance in the world and all those historical tough times. We have experienced all of that. We have experienced the wheel of karma. Right now, we are more or less back in balance. We should feel more connected to everything.

Always be open to new and different perspectives but strong enough to know to ask questions and accept that you may hear something doesn't resonate with your expectations. You are awake when you completely heal yourself and find that inner peace. You know life's secrets and you know you are a soul in a flesh body. You are not attached to people or things. You just want to "be". Society 's pressure doesn't bother you, you feel pure, and you want to share peace, freedom and love. Enlightenment means recognizing the fact that all things are connected in the cosmos as they are interwoven together to reveal perceivable reality and the totality of all life in the universe.

When you're enlightened you no longer differentiate where you end and the universe begins. You just accept things as the one infinite creator. You recognize that your consciousness is borrowed from the source and therefore is shared as part of everything (people, animals, trees, plants, air, nature etc.)

Reaching a certain level of enlightenment, you will cease to have a physical body which is necessary condition for your existence. Be an eagle that sees everything below with clarity and escape from the limited reality to the eternal infinite wisdom and truth. Only you can see the exit. Remember the ant analogy mentioned before. You have unimaginable potential. We are the real ELITES. The so-called elites are the parasites and leeches who feed off our blood literally and metaphorically. Your DNA holds the treasure of all treasures.

AFFIRMATIONS

- I AM true to my purpose.
- My purpose is to Love everyone.
- My purpose is to love unconditionally.
- I will not get distracted by external nonsense.
- My mission is close to completion.
- My inner truth is all that matters.
- I AM awakening to my inner truth.

38

EGO/SOUL - YIN/YANG

Your higher self does not judge, compare, or demand that you defeat or be better than anyone. Don't let anyone define who you are. Discover your own identity and let your presence reveal your true self. Until the ego evolves to become one with your true self, you will remain a slave to your own ego. Being ego driven in your life is living in a dumbed down reality of the real thing as opposed to being soul driven. Egotistical people are the major gossipers. Remember that rumors are carried by haters, spread by fools and accepted by idiots. Distance yourself from fools that spend their time gossiping.

A spiritual awakening is not usually pleasant. It often feels like confusion, frustration, anger, sadness, or being out of place. A spiritual awakening can be uncomfortable and challenging because it is an intense time of personal growth. Despite how difficult it may feel, you are not going crazy, you are evolving. You are considered crazy only to those that haven't gone through the awakening process yet. Your soul has reincarnated many times.

Here are some signs :

You see through illusions very easily.

You are an extremely sensitive person.

You have a very strong intuition.

You may feel like you don't belong here (but you do- it is difficult for a reason because the soul is growth received in this dimension is massive).

You crave a deep connection and deep conversations with people who are good for you.

You have a high level of respect for nature, animals, other humans and everything in nature. Things like talents and gifts come to you easily because you have practiced them in other lifetimes. You tend to require a lot of time alone to recharge. Don't fall for your ego driven desires.

When you are aligned with egoistical vibrations, you will tend to think that you are sinning while you could be in the process of entering the right path. Recognize the duality of yin/yang-soul/ego. Adam and Eve are allegories for the yin/yang principles within you. The journey is to balance these energies. The forbidden fruit was the orgasm (and the carnism). The gateway to Eden is through congregation of sexual alchemy.

This is known as the great Arcanum, the secret teachings of tantra hidden within all religions. Learn to love your Light half, your Dark half, and the shades of gray in between so you can have a balanced whole being. Be yourself wherever you are. Don't agree to things to keep the peace. That's a trauma response. When you do this, you are disrespecting your boundaries.

Be decisive and say to yourself, "No more making myself uncomfortable for others to feel comfortable". You have the ability to control yourself. You can run your life instead of running it down. Be balanced. Do good and if you mistakenly do bad then it's important that you recognize the deed and improve next time. Don't think of it as a sin if you were to do something that would be seen as a negative from society. There is no such a thing as sin. People do good and bad things. Sin is a myth.

The concept of sin was created as a recruitment method to get people to join an immoral religious organization and to extort money from them. Religious leaders and believers tell you that you have an imaginary problem and coincidentally, they have a magic cure for your imaginary problem. When you align with your higher self, you won't fall for your ego's tricks. Work on your shadow self. Your shadow self is a part of you that carries all of your traumas and negative patterns accumulated throughout your life. It is the part of you that you try to keep hidden from the world and from yourself.

Little do you realize that connecting to and embracing your shadow becomes a very crucial step in the healing process. You have to be able to admit that you have (we all do) negative patterns of thinking and behaving before you can heal them. Once you can admit this, your awareness of your own behavior will become much more apparent and you will be able to objectively see where you are stuck and messing up.

Shadow work is the epitome of true accountability. Unless you do the shadow work, you will always be confused and not know how and why the things that happen in your life happen the way they do. You are here to innerstand yourself, your purpose and not to be innerstood. Nobody can innerstand you because only you can know you and that is through the shadow work. Which one will you feed, the Ego or the Soul?

Your **EGO**   Your **SOUL**

Seeks to serve itself	Seeks to serve others
Seeks outward recognition	Seeks inner authenticity
Sees life as a competition	Sees life as a gift
Seeks to preserve self	Seeks to preserve others
Looks outwards	Looks inward
Feels lack	Feels abundance
Is mortal	Is eternal
Is drawn to lust	Is drawn to love
Seeks wisdom	Is wisdom
Enjoys the prize	Enjoys the journey
Is cause to pain	Is cause to healing
Rejects God	Embraces God
Seeks to be filled	Is eternal wholeness
Is me	Is we
Once everything falls into place, I will feel peace	When I find peace, everything falls in place
~ ~ ~	~ ~ ~

When the ego dies, the soul awakes.

- I AM not my ego and that is not who I really am.
- I will not let ego thrive for approval, because I AM already aligned with my soul.
- My ego speaks in words while my soul speaks in silence.
- My ego is my soul's worst enemy.
- I remove the E from EGO and let it GO.
- My soul is my ultimate prize.

39

DIFFERENT JOURNEY SAME DESTINATION

"The spiritual journey is the unlearning of fear and the acceptance of love"

Your journey is not the same as mine or your family or anyone else's. We all meet each other on certain paths. There are an infinite number of paths crossing each other multiple times throughout your life's journey. You decide which path you choose. Some paths are faster but can finish on a dead end and some others are slower with turns and curves. It may take you to the destination sound and safe but it will take longer to get there.

Picture yourself and many others climbing a mountain. There are many paths to the destination which in this analogy is the summit of the mountain. Some paths to the top are soft curving but longer and some paths are shortcuts in the form of steepness or climbing from the dangerous rocky part of the mountain. There is a time for everything so if you hurry and try to force your way against divine timing, you most likely will exhaust yourself to the point of breaking down or falling off the cliff.

If you trust in yourself and divine timing then you will reach the destination safely with lots of experience and with minimal or no struggling. Don't think that you will reach the destination in this lifetime if you refuse to work on yourself. It may take you many lifetimes. You can focus on improving your life every step you take without causing harm to yourself and others. If you do, do not think you can escape judgement. The judgement I AM talking about is "**bad karma**". There is no God to punish you.

*Only your thoughts and actions punish (**bad karma**) or reward (**good karma**) you. If you stop here and there during the journey, you will slow down the progress.*

Many times I was trying to wake people up to the point that it felt like I was insisting. I was wrong. It was only suppressing my journey. Like my friend Joe said :

"It's not only your own journey, everyone has their own mission (journey) to fulfill".

Plus, I was enforcing others a way of inner standing that they were not yet ready to grasp. That is fine when you let someone know your point of view and let them decide whether to pick up on your message or not. But when you try to force your opinion on them, you might even hurt them. Everyone only inner stands what their mind is capable of at that moment.

Teaching must be gradually and incrementally or else you may trip just like if you were to make a child run when the child can only crawl. For the child to run, they first must walk and then run. It takes time to crawl then it takes time to walk before being able to run.

YOU WILL GET THERE.

GO AT YOUR OWN PACE.

Trust your instinct. Trust your gut. Trust your inner voice. Trust yourself. You will get there. Just don't stumble along the way. Never let anyone put you down. And if someone does, you get up stronger than ever. You have it in you. All of us do.

TRUST

YOURSELF

40

SUBCONSCIOUS – ABRACADABRA

Abracadabra is a phrase in Hebrew that means, "**I will create as I speak**". Only speak if it's better than your silence. The words you speak are the spells you are casting. That's why it's called "spelling". You can attract anything based on your thinking. If you are someone that complains a lot, you're going to keep complaining and you will attract people of the same mindset. It's an addiction that immobilizes you. If you are true to yourself and vibrate only in love, then you will live a wonderful life and will attract people of the same mindset.

I'm true to myself and when I encounter complainers or negative people, they weed themselves out of my life for me. I don't even need to tell them. To vibrate in love, you first must love yourself. By loving yourself, you know your worth and you don't need anyone else's approval. By not needing anyone's approval, you are truthful to yourself, others and your life will shine. You become the captain of your ship.

You decide the direction that your ship will take, toward calm smooth open waters full of possibilities or toward the direction of the storm that you will be engulfed in and thrown toward a cliff. You are the programmer of your mind. Your life is essentially a printout of your subconscious mind. What are the programs in your mind?

> Look at your life, the things that come to you and things that you want, come to you because you have programs in your subconscious that encourage them being there. Anything you struggle with, anything you have to work hard at, anything you put effort into, you are doing it because you are trying to overcome a program of limitation that is preventing you from getting out of there.

If you want to change and choose a different direction in life you must overcome those limitations that are keeping you hostage. You can't tell your subconscious mind to record anything, because it is not there. Your subconscious is just a player, unless you catch your subconscious those **two times** where it changes profession, from *player* to a *recorder*. Those **two times** (profession/function change) are, 1- Before bed and 2- As soon as you open your eyes in the morning. You must engage in hypnosis/ habituation regularly to the point that you will be in charge of your life and you will be mindful every step of the way. Yes, you have that power.

As far as I know there are three ways how to reprogram your subconscious:

1- From the age 0-7.

2- In your sleep while the brain is in **THETA** waves (any age after 10).

3- While conscious/awake, which out of all three is the most difficult one.

Let's look at all three and explore how to reprogram, how to chisel away what doesn't serve you and keep/add what is useful to you and the ones around you. If you don't, you will keep chasing your tail and be always confused.
Being confused will only slow you down or make you go step backwards in your journey. It is all a journey. Life is a school, a journey. Either you pass the grade or not. Apply the school analogy to life.

Pass the grade or not.

The ability rests within the will and determination that you apply throughout your everyday life.

41

CONSCIOUS PLAYER- SUBCONSCIOUS RECORDER

Your life is an expression of the programs installed in you. Over 90% of your life comes from your subconscious. Can you imagine the possibilities in your life if your subconscious matched your wishes, desires and aspirations you hold in your conscious mind? Twice a day your brain has the capability to download information and these two times are when you can reprogram your subconscious. If you learn and put into practice the system of how your subconscious records, then you will live the life you want.

The conscious mind being creative can learn from reading a book, watching a documentary, or listening to a lecture. Your conscious mind being creative has an unlimited way of downloading information but the conscious and subconscious minds are not connected in the sense that if the conscious mind learns something, it doesn't mean that the subconscious mind is learning it as well. Your conscious mind learns through its creative process and your subconscious mind learns primarily through two ways.

The subconscious mind is a habit mind. The two ways to download programs or habits in the subconscious mind are:

ONE
We download information into the subconscious mind in the first 6-7 years of life. The information can be downloaded straight into the subconscious mind when in theta brain wave or hypnosis state. In the first 6-7 years of life, a child's brain is predominantly operating in theta hypnosis and a child's brain records everything he/she hears. It is particularly important that you know this so you can teach your children the right things from the start.

I have heard many parents swear or say all kinds of horrible things in front of their children. They don't realize that after the first 7 years the child will start showing their parents traits. When you go to the doctor for a mental or emotional problem, the doctor will ask you about when you were a child and if there was a bad history in the family.

That's because it will show up later in life. We all have been subconsciously programmed as all of us parents have programmed our children to a certain degree. Unknowingly though. We did not know any better. Now we know. For the next time you have another child or if you don't have any more children, at least you can arm someone else with this information. This was one of the two ways to program the subconscious. You are not a child anymore so what is the other way to program it if you are an adult?

TWO

Twice a day your brain goes through a period of Theta vibrational activity. Twice a day your brain is prepared to download information through hypnosis. When you are sleeping, you are at the lowest vibrational frequency called Delta. When you are about to wake up or when you are about to fall asleep, they are two times where your subconscious brain records information. That's when you are in the dream world and you are mixing the two. This period is called Theta, where hypnosis occurs, the recording process.

As you become more awake, Theta goes to a higher vibration called Alpha. That's a calm consciousness. You start doing your morning routine while being calm and maybe getting ready to leave the house. By the time you get to work or anywhere where there are noises or people, your brain ramps up from Alpha (calm consciousness) to Beta brain waves which is the brainwave we operate in when we engage in a busy working environment.

Before you get into a hypnosis state before bedtime, listen to affirmation programs and guided meditation. You can choose specifically guided meditation music tracks. For example, if you want to have prosperity you can play the meditation that is for that desire. You can listen to a guided meditation program that is about peace of mind or any other type of healing music. And leave the music on all night. The hardest method to reprogram subconsciousness is during everyday life while conscious. You must be mindful every step of the way which is very difficult.

It is easier to reprogram your subconscious first before going to bed with affirmations, meditation and while asleep. Whatever music you have on all night will go into your subconscious, especially when you are in Theta mode. Search on the internet for subliminally recorded messages so you can reprogram your subconscious.

Or you can record your own using your voice if you want. Do not let anyone that you have disagreements with record it for you (assuming you would do that because that person may have a soothing voice to record). The reason you should not let that person do it is because you and her/him have an energetic contract. If that person has negative feelings toward you, it will transfer to you through her recorded voice. Program your mind instead of letting others program it for you.

You are your own recorder and player. Be careful of what gets recorded in your subconscious while you are not living in the moment.

Everything you see or hear gets recorded automatically in your subconscious. Beware of the kind of people you hang around with. Choose carefully the information you receive through books, Tv, internet etc. Being healthy is not only what you eat but also what information you consume.

Breathe deep. Hold your breath for a few seconds then slowly release. Repeat this a few times a day so you can be in the moment and live your life instead of just existing. You deserve better. You are the signature of the **CREATOR**.

REFLECT, PAUSE, BE STILL

By being still it means to still your mind. It means to calm your mind by being away from noise, opinions and redundancy. It means to practice daily solitude for at least one hour a day and stay away from noise so you can actually hear yourself. Instead of replaying corrupted scenarios in your head from too much intermingling with people.

Be careful what you think, say or do. Or else it might come back to you.

The moment you stop being mindful daily is the moment you pass the wheel to your subconscious. During your daily life you just replay old memories and habits. You trap yourself in a hamster wheel effect.

If you want to have the wheel back and be in charge of your life then be mindful and creative every step of the way. Always be willing to learn new things daily.

The idea we humans can only only 10% of our brain is total nonsense. When you do new creative activities daily, you create new neural pathways in your brain and a little at a time you expand and use way more pathways than 10%. Compare yourself with the version of you from years ago. Your brain capacity has expanded greatly, hasn't it? Meditating is crucial to unlocking your pineal gland and your right brain hemisphere. Be a player only when you record (in your subconscious) what really matters.

42

THE END IS THE BEGINNING AND THE BEGINNING IS THE END

"Life is your companion, death is your friend. When you embrace them both, you will realize that there is no beginning and that there is no end"- Saimir Kercanaj

The supposed fact that there is a beginning and an end is just a concept seeded into your mind by society. You are constant, continuous, infinite energy and energy never ends. Energy just transforms. Yesterday, today and tomorrow are not consecutive, they are connected in a never-ending cycle. Everything is connected with everything. "**I**" is **Alpha**, "**AM**" is **Omega**. Stay focused on the source "I" and on the manifestation "AM". "I AM" is one of God's names and points at the transcendence nature of the Creator.

This God is not a man with a bird head, ox head, bull or a serpent. " I AM " is bigger than any of that. God is also referred to as " Alpha and Omega" , referring to the first and last letter of the Greek alphabet. The beginning of all things and the ultimate end of them. A focus on "the end" leads to anxiety and self-destruction.

Think of how many religious people fixate on nothing but "hell". Keeping our focus on the beginning and the glory of the Creator, enables us to let that Light and Love flow through us. Transforming us into a spring of living water and allowing us to draw closer to the cosmic throne in the here and now. This is what it means for the Kingdom of God to be at hand.

Physical life is not forever but your soul is. It's all cyclical. If you die tomorrow, do you think you will live forever? Of course not. Not in the physical sense. Not as this person you are now. You will reincarnate as another person. You will die and be reborn constantly. Your soul won't die. It is eternal. Our three-dimensional perceptive mind cannot grasp such states of being while conscious on earth.

When you meditate, dream, astral travel or die, you will grasp and experience these states of consciousness. You must be ok and accept that you are temporarily here. This is all you have so make the best of it. When you look death in the eyes, you will realize that there is no reason to worry or fear dying. I suggest you have a romantic relationship with death. I do.

A few years ago, when a friend of mine told me that he had a romantic relationship with death, in my head I was thinking "get away from this guy, run as fast as you can". I did not innerstand him at that time but little by little I was winking at death and death was winking back. And the more I embraced and accepted death as a part of me, I stopped being afraid of dying. I was even picturing a big 10 story high tsunami wave while driving on a highway many times. It felt good to not feel afraid of dying. When you know death, you become best friends. It doesn't mean that I don't care if I die.

It just means that I appreciate life and enjoy the moment because whenever death arrives, it will still be a new present moment. There is no reason you should fear dying. Don't be scared that you will die forever. Only you (*your name and your physical body*) will die forever. Your ego, your lower self will die but not your spirit. I am telling you from pure raw experience/truth and common sense. The moment you stop fearing death, is the moment you begin living. The more you stay away from facing the fear of dying, the more your fear will take your life away. Not only will it destroy you mentally and emotionally, but you will bleed your drama and depression on those that have not done anything wrong to you, especially your children. When you elevate your soul to the Supreme Omnipotent Being level "Alpha/Omega, then you have learned how to avoid death, live for eternity and undergo the metaphorical change.

This will ensure all your past lives are uploaded to your current one. Have you ever wondered whenever there was someone that seemed to have a dead-end life, they turned it around fast? That's because on a subconscious level, they get a big nudge by their soul or higher self. Many souls want to be here and learn.

Your soul nudges you all the time through people you come in contact with daily or through dreams, specific situations that you find yourself in a position to have to choose between a good or bad action. There are situations where the soul gets tired from you neglecting life constantly. When your soul has had enough, you may die as a result of a disease or an accident. You cannot blame the food industry for selling junk food, because you had the choice to eat healthy. Your soul messages you from a higher perspective where it is not limited by the five senses. You are limited while conscious but limited only when you are not in alignment with your soul. Life is your companion, death is your friend and when you embrace them both, you realize that there is no beginning and that there is no end. Reflect on that.

What is the END? It is just a new BEGINNING.

It is a never ending journey that serves as a lesson for you so you can be catapulted into the depth of your soul and realize who you really are.

Begin or Start
It is a form of art

43

ETERNAL SOUL DRESSED IN MATTER

"You exist in time, but you belong to eternity. You are a penetration of eternity into the world of time. You are deathless, living in a body of death. Your consciousness knows no death, no birth - It is only your body that is born and dies" -Osho

Y our soul cannot live completely in the body because it would die (the body). What happened to you and many others is in the head. The mind is extremely complicated for us to innerstand. It all happens in the mind, as in the Universal Mind with all of the countless dimensions. Our physical brain is just a tool so God/Universal Mind can experience and expand itself. Your physical brain is the cd player and the mind(quantum field/ether) is the cd/software. There is much confusion about souls leaving bodies or entities taking over souls and so on. I am being drawn to clear up much of this confusion and distortion within these ideas.

First and foremost we must innerstand our (physical body) is a mere pattern of energy/frequency. (Physical reality) is contained within a Spirit, a projection of a Spirit, in a sense, not the other way around. We do not have bodies or souls, we ARE soul/spirit. The body is a smaller physical projection and a representation of the Greater soul-matrix to a degree. The body cannot exist without a soul because "THE" spirit is what creates matter. Consciousness is what creates reality. Your soul cannot leave or detach from your body or be taken over by another entity etc.

All of these experiences are created by our mind and our 'belief systems' as a means to cope and 'make sense' of what is going on within our mind/body/spirit complex. This can most definitely make things 'appear' and 'feel' as if those things mentioned above are what is occurring but mechanically speaking, this is not what is actually happening.

The truth is that it is the Spirit that creates/co-creates the body/reality/experience. And I know this can be a challenging concept to grasp for some but it's simply how reality works, the physics of it, the mechanics of it. How

Light filters through us, is how we 'perceive' the reality, that will make the most sense to 'us', because very rarely we see it for what it truly is and what is actually occurring on a fundamental level which only really occurs when all our filters are removed/dissolved. Many would call this "Enlightenment" or **Buddhahood.**

Fundamentally, you cannot be touched but you can buy into the 'beliefs' to create an 'experience' for yourself that makes it 'seem' as if you can for whatever reason it may really serve you. Based on our reality, it is not really what is actually, mechanically happening. The only thing that can happen to make people 'think' they are an entirely new soul or persona is that the mind/ego and 'false sense of selves' experience their own illusion and/or death. We surrender and merge with the greater self/soul so to speak. We now embody a greater degree of our entire soul-matrix (i.e., walk-ins/awakenings etc.) but you can never lose or leave your soul/body etc.

These (the explanation of the above paragraph) are all illusions of this immensely powerful creative tool we call (The Mind) that many of us have not been trained to use properly and allow to run amuck and become the master of our reality when it was never designed to be the master but rather the skillful servant. In your sleep, you are sometimes connected with spiritual guides or teachers from other realms. Also, while awake, your inner being is your true teacher. We also must innerstand that what we hold onto and identify ourselves with like our 'thoughts, feelings and beliefs' is what most directly reflects into the reality we experience.

And in a sense, traps us in the illusion of time, mind and space and keeps us slightly in the past/future because we are still holding onto things rather than being truly present. Learning to let go births the inner standing that we are a new greater being, still you, but more you, each and every moment. It is much easier said than done. These words don't come out of thin air. I AM reminding you so maybe someday you can may remind me or our future generations or vice versa. This is how we walk each other home by cutting through the New-Age 'Spiritual Fluff' with basic and fundamental/universal laws & principles. The Microcosm reflects the Macrocosm. What is occurring within you also reflects on the external reality/experience because Inner = Outer.

As Above So below. As within so without. As the universe so the soul.

You already know this but may have temporarily forgotten. You are an eternal soul dressed up in matter (flesh, skin, bones etc.). When you die, you will change different clothes the higher you go, to the point that dressing up will not be required anymore. You will be naked as in "energy". Anytime you have difficulty inner standing or accepting a concept that is far beyond your grasp, compare it with lesser forms. By lesser, I don't mean in an egotistical/condescending way that you are better. They are considered lesser from our point of view. They are just as important as we are. And those things are for example Elementals.

Do the elementals innerstand the rocks?
Do the rocks innerstand the plants?
Do the plants innerstand the animals?
Do animals innerstand humans ?
Do humans innerstand souls ?
Do souls innerstand the Prime creator/cosmic intelligence?

The answer is **yes** to all these questions. One of the questions can be answered with "NO" by many of us because we have lost the ability to know by default our soul, collective consciousness and everything that exists physically or metaphysically.

At one point in time, we were united with all life forms. I could have very well skipped all the metaphysical subjects in this book but then the book would be half complete and showing you only one side of the coin. You will never have a clear mind and peace of heart unless you innerstand the metaphysical part of yourself. The metaphysical doesn't only mean after death or in your dream while unconscious or while deep meditating. You cannot see your thoughts or your feelings therefore these are also metaphysical.

It is very important to take your existence seriously and work on your emotions and thoughts also. We live our everyday life by paying attention to only what we physically see and we ignore the importance of our thoughts and emotions.

Our emotions and thoughts become physical in the sense that our everyday actions and behavior happen as a result of our thoughts and emotions which are both metaphysical aspects of our body. And we have power over them while conscious. You (most people) have been trained to think that you are useless, a mistake and that you are not intelligently designed. You and hundreds of generations before you have been trained to believe that, so that the schemers can keep controlling and living off your fear, anxiety, worry, lack of abundance etc. It is all a lie. There is an abundance of everything. Your DNA is the universal alchemist. Talk to it.

> *Your DNA is like a genie in a bottle except they are genes in your body. Connected to the unified field of the universe, they react to your thoughts to make your wishes a reality by attracting people, things and experiences which you desire and think about most. Your DNA is your soul roadmap for where you have been energetic wise.*

Your DNA is a record of your past (in our linear way of inner standing TIME) incarnations during multiple phases of existence and parallel realities. From where you sit, the DNA is a testament to your evolutionary and karmic relationship with the universe. Maybe you don't quite innerstand it and have written off 95% of it as junk because you have yet to recognize it's truth and purpose.

The physical bodies are needed before the ascension process as they are carbon-based. After the ascension, there is not a physical body anymore but only a hologram. It's a holographic projection that you can create with your mind so that others can see you. Don't forget that the light at the end of the tunnel is not an illusion. The tunnel is an illusion. The tunnel is a false construct created by your Ego/beliefs.

AFFIRMATIONS

- I AM an eternal heavenly being and death is non-exist ent in my consciousness.
- I AM dressed up in matter and belong to infinite eternity.
- I AM not scared of death and my soul doesn't recognize it.
- My outside makeup (physical vessel) is only temporary.

- My physical body is my temporary costume.

- My higher self guides me at all times.

- I AM eternal energy and dressed up in matter.

Death is just an illusion. Your flesh is simply the outer shell. You are a multidimensional being.

"You are eternal, your body is temporary. Death does not end all. Death does not mean total annihilation. Death does not end the chain or sequence. The working agent, the Soul in the body, does not and cannot die with the death of the body. One's soul is immortal. Just as a person lays aside their coat, so also one lays aside the physical body at death". - Sivananda

44

3D - 5D AND BEYOND

W hat is 3D? 3D stands for three dimensional. This is the three-dimensional reality that we have been living in on this Earth since the beginning of this matrix prison that was created to keep us suppressed and separated from the source. It is an indisputable fact that there are other dimensions out there. In your dreams you are in a different dimension. When you astral travel or lucid dream you find yourself in a different dimension.

After you die you will be in a different dimension. Deja vu is a different dimension, regardless if Deja vu happens as a result of past lives, memories or parallel timelines overlapping each other. Our world is three dimensional. We operate in a space-time continuum and our space is that of three dimensions, height, width and depth.

Everything we come in contact with, every object we touch and everything we know, we perceive them as having these three geometric dimensions. We live in a prison or in a box governed by parameters set in place by our five senses and our limited experiences and the way we perceive our world in these three geometric dimensions. When you realize that other dimensions exist, you will never think of this reality we are living in the same way again. After that realization, Life and death have different meanings then what you were taught since birth. Our three-dimensional world is a world of duality. We operate within these duality concepts such as, in/out, left/right, up/down, can/cannot, love/hate etc. Our way of perceiving reality is a distorted reality of survival, control and competing with one another.

Our three-dimensional reality has two possibilities. Whichever possibility anyone belongs to will depend on the level of spiritual consciousness of every individual.

Possibility 1 exists for those that if they can see it, touch it, taste it or smell it then they can prove that it exists and so in their level of consciousness that reality is real. Anything beyond what they can perceive as real gets screened out by their lower self or Ego and they will dismiss any other possibility as fantasy or delusion and cognitive dissonance will kick in. They are right in their own level of inner standing because they perceive only the manifested world.

Possibility 2 is the non-manifested world that exists within us. And that is the spiritual dimension or reality. Or the fourth dimension. The majority of humans live in the manifested world or the visible reality. They live in a world of duality, a world of illusion, a linear time life path where they are constrained by the limitations of the visible three-dimensional world. The non-manifested world reality or 4D is a frequency band , another dimensional reality. There are three dimensional beings in 4D reality where they don't have the constraints that we have here .

The 4th dimension is not somewhere else. It is here where we are but we don't see it because as I mentioned before it is a frequency band. A perfect example to describe it is by thinking of the radio. We hear the music on one channel but within the same 3d physical radio there are other channels occupying the same space. It's the same for the 4D world. We can't see it with our own physical eyes but it exists in the same world that we live in.

You cannot travel to 4d by conventional ways of traveling like in a car or in an airplane. It is not separate from our world. The only way to travel in 4D is through portals or doorways of consciousness in two ways. The first guaranteed way to travel in 4d is by death of the physical body, where our soul gets released and through through portals into a higher dimension than the three-dimensional world.

The second way to travel there, which I can confirm because I have travelled in 4d many times is through meditation, lucid dreaming, astral travelling, near-death experience or OBE (out of body experience). The only experience that I haven't had is "near death experience", otherwise I have been in 4d through all other ways mentioned above. Beside the first way which is guaranteed to reach 4d through physical death, it is guaranteed also through the second way but only when you're not locked predominantly into the 3d world constraints.

So, anyone can travel in 4d. Travelling in different dimensions happens when your mind enters an altered state of consciousness or reality and it splits from your physical body. By "your mind", it means the invisible energy. Your mind is not physical. Your brain is physically the tool that the mind needs to express itself. By meditating regularly, anyone including you can travel in different higher dimensions. The timeline split has already happened. Where a decision has been made for the advancement of earth.

Earth is moving up in 5d. Meaning a new Earth is being created. Not another earth beside us or somewhere else in the universe, but it occupies the same place we are now but in 5-dimensional frequency. Just like the difference between 3d and 4d where beings from both dimensions cannot interact with each other physically without going into altered states of consciousness but also between 3d and 5d will apply the same scenario. Keep in mind the radio analogy mentioned previously. We are skipping 4d altogether.

One reason based on my research is that the low vibrational satanic corrupted soul entities are stationed in the lower astral realm of 4d. That is the only place where they can communicate with their minions in 3d.

The minions I'm talking about are higher up politicians, major religions leaders, specific elite members where they gather and perform rituals on specific days of the year so they can communicate with those other worldly entities in 4th dimension.

There was always war between the forces of dark and light. And between the bad ETs (extraterrestrials) and good ETs. It is your choice to believe if there are otherworldly species or not. If you are already a spiritual person then you already know that they exist. We are also extraterrestrials in their eyes. Terra from Latin means land, extra terra= extra land.

We use the word extraterrestrial for every kind of alien, from the supposed space, assuming it is real. Since extraterrestrials mean those that are from extra land, it doesn't necessarily mean that they are from a different planet. Maybe extraterrestrial means where we think our world ends. Maybe there is more land? Hmm, maybe you should ask the question, why are we NOT allowed to go to the South Pole, or the North Pole. Whatever news you may have seen of the fake prince or expedition teams that went to the south pole, it is fake. The _behind-the-scenes shadow goverment_ does not allow anyone to go there. The extra land continues as in stretching out where our land supposedly ends, based on the fake map. Or maybe the land continues inside the Earth from both the outer pole and central pole, or north and south pole for those that beLIEve that we live on a round Earth.

Maybe there are civilizations inside the Earth. Maybe? Who am I kidding? There ARE civilizations inside the earth. Always were. When Atlantis was destroyed and when the flood happened and many other times where catastrophic incidents happened, people and other ET races moved into the inner Earth. Think Agartha or Shambala. Maybe Agartha exists in 5D. Something to think about. Like I was saying earlier, the time split has already happened. The drama currently unfolding on Earth is scripted and is occurring precisely because the divergence is near. At the point of the switch between old and new Earth, the 3d programs will continue but in another theater. Meaning, in another Earth (of another frequency/reality).

If you vibrate with total love and compassion, you will move on to 5d. You will be on the same Earth that you are now meaning on the same physical Earth but you will be living a life of bliss where peace, freedom and love reign everywhere. That would be 5d frequency. But If you live in fear, worry, hate, lack etc then you will move into the other 3D earth or plane. You will die normally before this divergence happens and you will reincarnate again in 3d. But not in the near future "5d Earth", or you will incarnate on another low dense 3d plane/reality.

If you are still alive at the point of the divergence, you will get sick and die anyway because your body will not be able to handle the Light that will penetrate the whole Earth. As some you might already know, Earth will go through a big energetic wave or a photonic belt. It has already entered the energetic belt, hence the great awakening where more and more people are awakening.

It's not a coincidence. The awakening is happening because the Earth and everything in or on it is bombarded with Gamma light rays which means we should be very happy there are otherworldly beings that care about us. It might pose the question that if they care about us then why make us suffer for thousands and thousands of years?

One reason is, because just like we have seasons (sun, greeenery, winds, rains and colds) on Earth, there are also seasons in the universe where there are a few hundreds or thousands of years of darkness, but also centuries and millenia where there is happiness, peace and freedom. Every few thousand or so years we move into a new age. We left the age of Pisces and we already entered the age of Aquarius. Aqua means water and water is smooth, clear and unified. The age of Aquarius is like that. That's what 5d Aquarius age or NEW AGE (don't confuse the fake new age propaganda that has infiltrated our times) is about. A life of bliss and no more suffering. It will be a life of love, care and compassion. We will not use watches or clocks anymore.

There will be an abundance of everything. My suggestion is for you to let go of everything negative that has plagued our society. Don't think for a second that if you die you will reincarnate in the beautiful 5d world.

You will only incarnate in the same 3d dense low energy world if you don't heal all the wounds caused by this fake matrix. When you reincarnate in 3d again you will feel as if your consciousness has been ripped apart from the void and placed in a flesh prison (body) to suffer until you die.

This is how living in 3d is. All of us were born prisoners of this false matrix. Appreciate all life forms, love everyone unconditionally and you will reincarnate in 5d. If it happens that you are alive in the middle of the change from 3d to 5d or divergence, then all the memories of this brutal world will fade from your memory, minus a vague lingering sense that some kind of climatic narrative took place.

And rest assured that we will actually make contact with the benevolent ETs but only when you are vibrating high and vibrating in love frequency. Love frequency is the highest, therefore if you vibrate in love frequency it means that you are already 100% honest toward your fellow humans and otherworldly beings.

Vibrating in Love frequency doesn't only mean loving a woman or a man in an intimate way but by loving everyone unconditionally, your family, your friend, coworker, and anyone else you don't know. Technically you know everyone from other past lives or parallel realities. We are all star seeds. Don't feel disappointed when you hear others say they are star seeds.

> *Everyone is a star seed. We all come from the stars. It's just that some star seeds forget their mission when they incarnate here and fall for the 3d worldly desires.*

Our memories of past lives get erased. From the moment we are born we are considered Gods with amnesia. We have the signature within our DNA. We were created from star beings. Beings that are so advanced who can create any biological species.

Those beings reside in 5d and up. But they can go below their dimensions and change form. They can even go as low as 3d when they have an important mission for helping humanity ascend. Just like Jesus/Sananda (Sananda is Jesus's spiritual name) and other ascended masters that reincarnated on Earth to give a boost to humanity's consciousness.

Although Jesus (or Jashua or Sananda) made a huge impact, it still wasn't able to get people to ascend to 5d because we were not ready back when he roamed Earth. But now it's different. We have advanced in consciousness with the ascended masters' help of course from their higher dimensions. They have helped us through dreams, meditation and other ascended masters incarnated on earth by laying low and helping us all develop along.

As I was saying earlier, we will make peaceful contact with the ETs. And to be able to make that contact externally, you must first liberate and activate that ET that is within you. Meaning that star seed that is dormant within you and waiting to explode as soon as you light it up. Earth's frequency is rising. That frequency is called 'The Schumann resonance'. We are also rising, not all but many. The person reading this book is definitely rising in frequency.

We must all tune to Mother Earth's frequency. We have to. She will not wait for us. We had many thousands of years of chances to rise. Many people report hearing ringing in their ears. This is because we are rising in frequency just like Gaia/Earth. Many that don't hear the ringing yet, most likely is because they need to finish their mission here on earth.

> *Everyone who uses a physical body here on Earth (so called "School" in this plane of existence) are all subjected under the Law of Karma or Universal Law , hence you have to wait for your "Turn" to go back home as per Lord of Karma's decision.*

I have had ringing in the ears since the beginning of 2020. The ringing means that downloads are happening. Light codes (information/wisdom) are getting downloaded and the DNA is getting upgraded from carbon based to crystalline. By crystalline, I don't mean crystal or glass, I mean light encoded DNA. If you had a specific ringing regularly for some time, and then all of a sudden you hear another kind of ringing don't worry, it's just new light codes getting downloaded after you were accustomed to the previous one.

If you hear ringing in your ears, know that your consciousness is getting expanded. We should be incredibly happy and grateful that we are alive in these times of transition from 3d to 5d. You might ask yourself why be happy when we see struggle and tyranny all around us?

> *Try picturing yourself going up a hill and when you reach the top of the hill to go down the other side you will see that you will fly on your way down because there is no resistance, and you are lighter. Only when you know in advance where the finish line is, which is on the way down the hill, you are happy to be part of the race. The race is the path to full enlightenment, even though enlightment happens every day. As long as you progress, you become enlightened compared to the previous self.*

The same with the transition from 3d to 5d. Only those that know the outcome, celebrate being reincarnated in these times. We all were incarnated for this transition. It's that not all remember it. Remembering doesn't mean that you will remember actual words on a contract that you signed before reincarnating here. Remembering means feeling it in your heart.

That's why the age of Aquarius is all about knowing things without having to remember anything. Once you are in 5d you will never incarnate again in a duality matrix like the 3d low density vibratory Earth, unless you choose to incarnate in a lower dimension to help those people of the 3d world rise up. Just like all ascended masters that came from 5d, 6d and up to reincarnated on earth to help humanity.

We wouldn't be able to see those beings (from 5D and up) with our naked eyes. No more reincarnating in this duality Matrix. 1d are often crystals, trees, plants etc. It's consciousness and they have no soul. 2d are often animals who have a soul and newbie souls that just reincarnated on earth. Its again a level of consciousness. 3d Is the matrix around Earth and humanity.

At the moment humanity is at the level 3d of consciousness. 4d is often the realm of reptilian or the lizards (other alien races, ghosts, fairies, elves and the mystical realms).

5d is Earth without the matrix. 5d is often star seeds, lightworkers. Humanity gained that knowledge and raised the vibration. There are also alien races like the Pleiadeans, Lemurians who are empathic alien (extra terrestrial) races. The ladder of dimensions (realms/realities) goes way up to 6d, 7d, 8d, 9d, 10d and more dimensions. It's only a level of consciousness.

Knowledge if you like. For example, school where you have a group of students in the 1st grade then another group of students in second grade and so on.

While dreaming, meditating, astral travelling, having an out of body experience and when you die you experience different dimensions (levels of consciousness/realities).

Physicality is the lowest densest form of life for our kind.

45

CARBON TO CRYSTALLINE

We were trapped in this 3d dense prison matrix created by the malevolent ETs from hundreds of thousands of years ago. They operate this veil of matrix through the 4d dimension. We cannot see them. Not in this three-dimensional world we are living in anyway. They can be seen in your dreams or while meditating only if you operate in fear and if you are under the use of low vibrational substances such as alcohol. If you meditate, try to have not drank alcohol for at least a week. In my strong educated opinion, you should not consume alcohol at all.

I'm nobody to tell you what to do because you are a sovereign heavenly being living in a free will zone, although this free will zone called Earth is captured by the groups of ETs I mentioned previously. Don't feel let down. The low frequency imposed on us by them can be destroyed by the way you think and feel.

By vibrating in love, honesty, integrity, compassion, the three-dimensional matrix can be dissolved and it will dissolve. But the more people become in charge of their lives and say no to tyranny, the faster the matrix will dissolve. Every 26,556 years there is a Star Activation cycle that our DNA is linked to. Before the invasion and tampering of our DNA 300k years ago, Angelic Humanity had 12 strands of DNA which were keyed to the planetary grid and stargate system.

Organic Stargate is true Ascension. We are getting back or getting reactivated again, including the rest of our DNA threads. It's been a few years now that our DNA is getting upgraded. But because the missing threads (95%) of our real DNA has been dormant for that long, we must go through the process of awakening first or else we won't be able to withhold the energetic shift (3D-5D) that will soon happen.

For now, light codes (high gamma energetic rays from the central sun) get downloaded into us while dreaming and through meditation. They will be activated when the right time comes which depends on the day where we as a species have reached a certain frequency/vibration.

It will happen soon. Just love unconditionally, say no to tyranny, be your true self and it will come in no time. Do you think that millions of evolved souls would come to earth just to die in a totalitarian new world order? Absolutely NOT. We (you are one of the evolved souls) came to flip this world upside down back to its original state. We reincarnated here for the NEW EARTH, for world peace and freedom. For the immortal golden age, the new Eden. We came here for an intergalactic evolved society. You are the one that is paving the way for a new world of peace, freedom and prosperity. Don't be surprised if one day (could be within the years) you wake up and you know everything. Well, if you all of a sudden know everything, you wouldn't know that you knew nothing the previous day, would you? All of us have been constantly bombarded with gamma rays by the Galactic Federation. Some think that the Galactic Federation is fake. That's because reverse psychology has been played on them (extreme skeptics) since the beginning of the 90s when the cabal/dark forces infiltrated the movement of bringing to light the Galactic Federation.

When you read about something for a while, it may become your new belief. You could say that maybe I might have fallen for the opposite of reverse psychology. I think not. The reason for it is because when you put two and two together, you can see what has been happening is part of a plan that started a long time ago so we as a species wake up and realize who we are, where we came from. But for that to happen, our dormant DNA must be awakened.

> In the New Earth frequency our DNA will have 12 strands and 144.000 genes. Our DNA will be crystal and not carbon based. We will have a Light body. And that can happen by receiving light codes (gamma rays).

While you sleep you are receiving constant downloads. When the time arrives where the majority of people are ready to accept disclosure of other worldly (dimension species) entities, then the switch will be flipped on. That will happen when we (Earth gets bathed by the Gamma rays coming from the Sun) enter the photon belt properly.

> Only a small percentage of people living on this planet will go through a full ascension process after the Event (solar flash/photon belt). The vast majority will stay in the physical reality with carbon-based physical bodies although with many more choices and many more options.

The option will be available when there is no more action by the malevolent group of beings controlling the Earth. It will be a life without poverty and with new advanced technology. There will be technology merged with spirituality that can improve the structure of the cells so they can replicate better and organs can be more efficient.

You are shifting levels of consciousness. Here are a few signs:

1. You feel a strong need to move to a new house, quit your job or move to a new place because your environment no longer feels right.

2. You want to spend a lot of time alone. You no longer feel in harmony with your old life, friendships or environment.

3. You begin to experience periods of manifestation on demand, miracles and super flow as you experience your new vibration.

4. The world around you feels different as if you've stepped into a new reality.

5. You feel confused and uncertain but deep down you know something amazing and incredible is coming.

Your DNA is getting upgraded from carbon based to crystalline.

46

"I AM" IS THE KEY THAT OPENS ALL DOORS

"The kingdom of God is within you" -Leo Tolstoy

Inside the very center of the heart exists something amazing and much bigger than you realize. It is a small spark of the Divine that you carry in the sacred place of the heart, that will soon unite you with other like hearted and like-minded heavenly beings. It is a small spark and yet, it is the biggest in the universe when it gets activated. It will trigger an immense explosion of Light. The likes of which has never been seen on Earth throughout many hundreds of thousands of years that we have been under the influence of malevolent forces.

You are a multidimensional soul having an experience in a physical body. Carry this spark carefully, nurture it, breathe Love into it and know that you are part of the Universal Divine plan. That spark is the center of creation within you, within your Godself that created everything in the whole universe out of pure Love. You are travelling through different stages of spiritual awakening while transforming the distorted light/darkness into Light.

You are awakening to the truth. The truth that everyone yearns for. And that truth is the only universal truth for everyone. The purpose is how to be a true creator.

To be a creator you must be initiated and tested everyday mentally, physically and emotionally. You are part of the school that is called 'life'. Nothing comes easy here. There is no reason to be afraid. The lessons that you must go through are part of the enlightenment process. You got to shine light and the darkness will disappear. It has no choice. Try and turn the lights on in the house or a flashlight at night. You will see that darkness will easily disappear. If your flashlight's batteries are running low, then the darkness will be mixed with the light and it will be dim. It is the same thing of your life experience.

When you are not true to yourself, your desires, wishes, and good feelings will be mixed with over-thinking, lack of abundance or any other emotions or thoughts that will immobilized. You will be confused and won't know the path you are taking is toward the Light or the dark. Pay attention to the things you are naturally drawn to.

They are often connected toward your path, passion and purpose in life. Key word here is "naturally". Some that may be drawn to fake drama people, or drawn to materialistic nonsense, will think that's their purpose and their path. Instead, they will have a cloudy judgement and a closed heart. You would be lying to yourself if you thought that your purpose and path is that kind of distorted reality. Being drawn naturally means from your heart, from your inner being where that spark, that universe resides.

Take care of your four homes which are your body, mind, soul and Earth. You are here to rise up. You are here to become the alchemist who transmutes darkness into light and low vibrations to high frequencies. The frequency of Love is something every one can obtain by simply being YOU. You are not your body; YOU are in your body. Or simply put, the real YOU , your higher self is not your physical body.

Your memories are not only contained in your chemical, physical, hard drive brain but they are also contained in your soul or light body. That is how people actually are able to have past life memories. Otherwise, it would be impossible for a person to have past life memories in their physical brain when they were physically born into this life.

When you have that connection to your higher self-light body, you have access to those memories. Your physical body is inside your soul, inside your MER-KA-BA (Footnote #14). It is inside that Light energetic body that stretches a few meters in diameter outside of your physical body.

With your physical eyes you can only see your physical body and anything physical in this three-dimensional reality. If and when you are able to see with your spiritual eye (pineal gland or third eye), will you realize that your physical body is a very cheap version of the real YOU.

There is a limit to how much or how many things you can see with your physical eyes. To achieve that kind (spiritual insight) of sight, you first must align yourself with the one that you don't see, which is your other you, or better yet the real YOU, your higher self. Live your life to express and not to impress. Trying to impress others can only boost your ego. Become One with everyone and do not separate from the "whole".

An anthropologist proposed a game to children of an African tribe. He put a basket of fruit near a tree and told them that the first one to reach the fruit would win them all. When he told them to run, they all took each other's hands and ran together, then they sat together enjoying the fruit. When asked why they all ran together when one could have taken all the fruit for themselves. They said, "*UBUNTU*". How can one of us be happy if all the others are sad? "Ubuntu" is a philosophy of African tribes that can be summed up as

"I AM because WE ARE". The mother of all truths is that you are God (little God co-creator). If you cannot feel it or innerstand it, then go in front of the mirror to at least see with your physical eyes the key that opens all the doors in your life. The key that is responsible for having the ability to walk up the stairway to heaven (metaphorically speaking). You, me and everyone are in a play. As Shakespeare said:

"The world's a stage".

We are all actors. Every single one of us has a role to play. You can be a B actor, an A actor, the writer, director, all the above or you can just be an NPC (Non-Player Character). Being an NPC is just existing and not living your life. Which one are you, an NPC, or the actor, writer and director of your life where you vibrate at the highest frequency possible?
You can't ascend to higher states of consciousness if you only think about yourself. You must focus on your 'I AM'. Your Godself is I AM. "I AM" is within us all.

This has been known for thousands of years by shamans, mystics and ascended human beings of higher states of awareness. And science is proving it. Independent scientists that have consciousness and loving human morals. Not those $cientists that only care about personal gain and career advancement.

Anything you say after '**I AM**', you become it. Say it consciously every day and feel it when you say it. You will be surprised and it will confirm that you are aligning with your true self which is part of the whole creation. Part of Oneness. Practice the mantra or affirmation "I AM" in the language that you feel more comfortable speaking.

These two words "I AM" are embedded in the collective consciousness of the universe. That code or software is energy light code. Not English or German or any other language. When anyone says for example, "I AM healthy and lovable" in their own language, it has the same effect .

Although English is not my mother language, I feel more comfortable practicing affirmations in English. If you are Italian who speaks the Italian language then you would say " IO SONO" which translates to "I AM".

You get the idea for any other language that you may prefer practicing the affirmations. Read the "I AM" as it's spelled and not as " I'm". It is especially important that you read it as is. Read them with conviction. Feel them. The emphasis must be on the "A" vowel of the words "I AM" every time you practice any affirmation that has "I AM" in the sentence.

If you memorize them after a few repetitions, then you will have a faster result if you close your eyes and affirm them. And if it is dark in the room, even better so your pineal gland won't be disrupted by any artificial light. Your third eye is overly sensitive. It can even see the light of any devices you have close to you, such as the light of the numbers of a digital clock or any light no matter how dim it is.

Practice them every day and any time of the day. Practicing affirmations is a form of meditation. I purposefully wrote 7 affirmations at the end of the chapters plus writing the "I AM" in capital letters is what makes the difference. "I AM" is the *KEY THAT UNLOCKS ALL DOORS*. YOU are the **KEY** that unlocks all doors in your life. You hold the **KEY** to the ARK. You are also the ARK.

When you innerstand yourself it means that you have already lost the awareness of your mind and body. When this happens, the only thing that remains is pure consciousness. This is your true being/existence. Everything else is an illusion. You are pure consciousness. Your mind, body and any experiences that you have as a result of them is simply a lesson that you must pass and move onto the consciousness purity.

You are a spirit disguised in a meaty coat. Being a spiritual being is the way to live a fulfilled life. Spirituality is a round table where nobody can sit at the head of it, which means that nobody is the boss. They work toward the same goal that benefits everyone. Realize that you are a spiritual being, live your life in the highest genuine loving way that benefits you and those you come into contact with and watch how your life will be an amazing journey.

R.E.M.E.M.B.E.R

that you are:

STRONG when you know your WEAKNESS

BEAUTIFUL when you appreciate your FLAWS

WISE when you learn from your MISTAKES

"Time and space are moving in circles, know its law and you too shall be free. Free shall you be to move through the cycles, past the guardians that dwell at the door."
- From the EMERALD TABLETS OF THOTH

I highly suggest you read this book about the tablets that contain the mother of all knowledge. It is not a book for beginners though.

"I AM" AFFIRMATIONS

- I AM Love, I AM Light.

- I AM a divine being at all times.

- I AM perfect, I AM free.

- I AM everything I desire to be.

- I AM strong, I AM always me.

- I AM the Light that hits like a spear.

- I AM Divine and have no fear.

As you may now realize, the key to opening all doors was right at the beginning, in the title itself. Also, throughout the pages I wrote many times "I AM" in a specific way.

Do you know how many times your subconscious got bombarded by reading the "I AM"? The whole book had to be read which every time "I AM" was read, it was crucial to inner standing your life force creation since "I AM" is the most powerful mantra/statement in the universe. "I AM" is the key that opens all doors. You are the "I AM" presence of God that is the life force within every individual. You are the Godself. The source of creation.

Everyone is a Godself. Through our expressive experiences and behaviors, we fill the void, we finish the painting called life. You are a co-creator, a fragment of THE true creator embedded in you. Your Godself is responsible for every single thing that happens in your life.

> As a sovereign man or woman, you are king/queen of your kingdom which consists of your mind, body and spirit. You are the ruler of your kingdom and the mind control establishment (government) doesn't have the right to tell you what to do as long as you do not harm. The throne of your "king-dome" is located inside your skull which is the dome that houses your pineal gland. The pineal gland is also known as the seat of the soul or the holy seat. In other words, the pineal gland is the throne of your kingdom/king-DOME or temple of God which is located between the temples of your head.

You will realize that the kingdom of God is inside you and not outside. **All the answers are within**. You are the password that unlocks the puzzle. You are both the key and the treasure chest. You are the key that decides to take the **JOURNEY** to achieve absolute **PEACE** and **FREEDOM**.

ALL ANSWERS YOU SEEK,
ARE WITHIN YOURSELF.
DIG and FIND.

Zero travel requirement. Access them, embrace them, apply them.

YOU ARE THE KEY THAT OPENS ALL DOORS

I AM you; YOU are me.

We are all one big FAMILY

DAILY ASCENSION REMINDERS

T ype this list on your pc (or hand write it), print it and stick it on the wall where you have no choice but to see it when you wake up and during the day so you get reminded to do them. (Do as many of these as you can, if it's possible).

Breathwork-Inhale slowly for 5 sec or more until lungs are full, hold your breath for 5-7sec, release slowly for 5-7sec. Do the breathwork a few times a day at least.

Be in the moment. Be present. Conscious breathing always brings you to the present.

Sun gazing-At dusk and dawn, 10-15 sec every day.

Water intake-2-3 litres every day or more if needed.

Eye exercises-At least once a day.

Affirmations-Any time of the day. 3-5 times a day is particularly good. It is also particularly important to practice affirmations before meditation so you will fall easier in deep meditation.

Meditation-Before night sleep and when you wake up. If not possible twice, at least once is a must. At least a 15min session.

Listen to healing music -111hz, 432hz, 528hz etc. (avoid 440hz at all costs).

Physical exercise-Gym or the home treadmill, walk/run in nature.

Grounding-Walk barefoot on soil or grass whenever possible.

Shut off Wi-Fi-Before sleep, shut off the Wi-Fi and turn off your phone/tablet so the electromagnetic signals won't pierce your brain. If you need the device to listen to healing music while asleep, at least put it on airplane mode.

Fast-Every 2 weeks as a start. Then once a week. The day that you fast, drink only juices. No solid foods.

Gratitude-Practice gratitude every day. Write down 3-5 things you are grateful for.

Observation-Get used to observing things and don't engage analytically about things you have no control of.

Solitude-Be by yourself and away from everyone. Practice solitude so you can hear your real voice and not the outside noise. Solitude is the key to finding the keyhole in the dark.

BONUS MATERIAL

Poems, Quotes and Artworks
created by the author.

QUOTES

"When you master being silent, noise becomes nonexistent "

* * * *

"If you are happy, that is good, If you're unhappy that's also good. They both will take you to the same destination, just that one of them will break you before arriving there.

* * * *

"A habit repeated more than enough, will set you up for failure "

* * * *

" You want to be loved? Love yourSELF and the Universe must conspire to give it to you "

* * * *

" Life is your companion, death is your friend, when you embrace them both, you realize there's no beginning and there is no end"

* * * *

"Your mind is your home, if you have a messy home you will trip, if it is tidied up you will walk with ease and flow like a river. You have two choices, to self-destruct or to expand your consciousness"

* * * *

"When opinions guide your way, disaster grows day by day"

* * * *

"No matter how much energy you waste in memories and imagination, the only thing that matters is NOW"

* * * *

" There is always blooming from the darkness if you acknowledge it first. Deep within the depth of your heart there is the sparkle waiting to be ignited by you. Only you have the matches to light it up. Nobody can do it for you. "

LITTLE POEMS

I see Light, I hear a sound
I keep looking, but there is no one around
I changed my perception, I looked deep within
I asked myself: Where have I been?

I thought I was lost, I thought I had just died
And yet, there I was, standing right beside
Ego has been pulling me, been pulling me away
Just when I really needed, to save my beautiful day
I resisted with passion and finally became free
Then I realized that it was my higher self that saved me.

~~~

I AM deaf I AM blind, I AM free with a clear mind
I observe and let it be, I have no choice but to be me
I AM happy because I AM me
I AM part of this beautiful game, I AM life, the game's name.

~~~

Life is my companion, death is my friend
When you embrace them both, you will realize that
There is no beginning and there is no end.

~~~

I AM a divine being; my vision is crystal clear
No matter what really happens, I truly have no fear
I look up in the sky, and see birds fly around
I follow the source of the Light, and it is the Sun that I just found
The Sun shines on my shoulders and I enjoy the day

The warmth is felt so deep inside of me, that my heart shows me the right way.

~~~

I AM not what people want me to be
I AM what I AM meant to be
I AM eternal life and mystery
I AM you and YOU are me
I AM brave, fearless and free
I AM everything I want to be
I AM the sacred Love that rests in me

~~~

I AM Love, I AM Light, I AM divine being day and night
I AM perfect I AM free, I AM everything I desire to be
I AM strong, I AM always me.

~~~

Is this the beginning or is this the end?
I think it is neither, don't you think my friend?
Life is just a movie, you got to play your part
As long as you are compassionate, life will bloom from your heart

You can find the treasure, the one inside your soul
If you are not judgmental, the Universe will give you 'THE' call
You are eternal being, condensed in pure energy
The more you look within, the more you become free.

Your magical love rises from the depth of your heart
You must openly embrace, both the Dark and the Light
Your powerful Love from the heart freely soars
You are a magical heavenly being, you are
the key that opens all doors.

ARTWORKS

Enjoy over 25 artworks, accompanied with philosophy/spirituality.

Love yourself unconditionally first. It is the only way for you to love others. Your heart can lead you, while your mind can definitely mislead you if you do not keep balance between them.

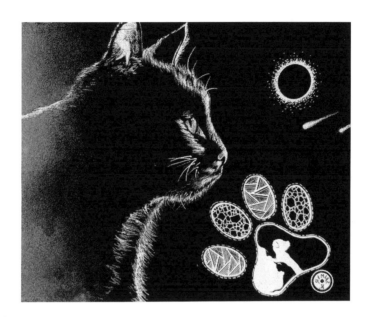

Animals are such agreeable friends. They ask no questions (at least from our way of innerstanding). They don't judge. You can better innerstand a life form by observing an animal than a human. The moment you observe a human being without judgement, is the moment you are every life form's friend. We are animals that speak in words. Our species happens to speak and think intellectually which has made humans become arrogant and egocentric. Observe animals and you will see how much you can learn from them.

There is a whole world inside and outside of you.

Be one with nature

Spend time in nature as much as you can so you can raise your vibration. You are part of nature. And nature is part of you. Imagine if trees gave off WIFI signals? If we planed many trees, we would heal mother Gaia/Earth and us much faster. **Too bad they** (the trees) **only produce the oxygen we breathe**. (sarcasm)

Dolphins have intelligence, intelligence with no end
If you vibrate high, you become their friend.

The key, where is the key? How far do you have to travel to obtain that mystery? Or is it closer than you may think? Or is it unreachable? I traveled for 35 years to reach the place where the key was. For many, it takes many lifetimes to discover it. You don't have to wait that many years, or months, or days. You can obtain the key today. At least take a peek at it. But with awareness, observation and practice you can definitely own it in no time, but only if you fight your demons (darkness within) first. What do you say?

As above so below, as within so without, as the Universe, so the soul.

*Remember, remember, the 5th of November (part of a quote from the movie). You might need to rewatch the movie "**V For Vendetta**" so you can take a dose of truth and fire from within.*

Look at the lake, look at the sun
Look at everything, life is just fun
No need to be afraid, life is just a play
Observe it with your heart, and live it day by day.

Is the time real? Kiss, and it will stop. Read and you will travel in time. Listen to the music and you can escape it. Write, if you desire to feel it. Breathe so you can release it.

You live in a mysterious world full of synchronistic encounters that are hints about your destiny. The more we wake up to this new world view, the faster we will create a completely new era that will manifest through our new way of heart/mind coherence. Not really a new way, it's the old true way, hidden from us. We will know things by default. No more getting stuck in living an analytical life.

No more needing to remember a thing. We will all have access to the same knowledge through the heart and paradise will be reached by all. In the old world there were only a few ascended masters. In the new one, every one can easily become an ascended master of self, since everything will be available. You can reach the peak of the mountain. Nobody can stop you because everyone is trying to reach it. Are you going to look within and find the entrance to PARADISE ?

In the next coming years I see an utopian world, spiritually in harmony where things like astral travel, telepathy, teleportation, levitation, clairvoyance, and telekinesis are as common as breathing. You may not believe this because you may think it is only possible what you understand (I used on purpose the word "understand and not "innerstand"). If you observe life philosophically and spiritually, you can clearly see that the superpowers mentioned above are very possible. Do you think the movies with super powers/superheroes are just a coincidence? The movies are full of truths, but only for those that have eyes to see and a mind to make sense of it (the truth).

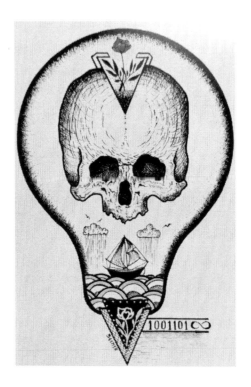

"*There is always life blooming from the darkness if you acknowledge it first. Deep within the depth of your heart, there is a sparkle waiting to be ignited by you. Only **YOU** have the matches to light it. Nobody can do it for you.*"

Love yourself. That is the most beautiful thing. When you love yourself, then you innerstand what true love is and in return you will love all life forms because you will know and feel what love is. Many people love others for personal gain. You are created to be loved. Things (objects) are created to be used. Don't love things. Don't use people, because that's the opposite of what everything was created for. You don't need to be accepted by others. You just need to accept yourself and everything else falls into place.

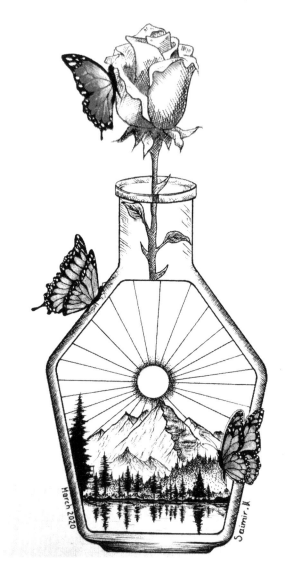

Fly, fly, fly free like a butterfly.
Do not be afraid, you will not die.

Opinions of others will only drive you off the cliff if you blindly believe. Use discernment. Listen to your own voice and not the noise imposed on you by others without your higher self's consent.

Who controls the moon? Other species, nobody, or our parallel universe selves? I think .....

Your body is your temple. Respect it. Nurture it. Reduce the amount of time that you talk about being ill. Refuse to allow illness a place in your consciousness. Consume fruit and vegetables. Some vegetables are pure medicine in the sense that they are very potent. For example "garlic". Garlic should be consumed only when you don't feel well. Should be used as a natural medicine. Your nervous system is very sensitive to Garlic. You wouldn't take medicine every day, would you? I used to consume garlic like crazy.

Since I reduced the amount that I consume, I AM not neurotic anymore. Garlic is a wonderful natural medicine. Organic is best and not the ones drown in fluoride. Spend time in nature. Clinical studies, raw experience in nature and common sense have proven that 1-2 hours of nature sounds a day, significantly reduces stress hormones up to 600-800% and activates 500-600 DNA segments known to be responsible for healing and repairing the body.

With a polluted mind, you will run in circles. Clear it of all the outside noise. Go within, in your heart and in your pine (pineal gland). It's where one of the treasures resides. It is within your reach. No need to travel at all. First you must be blind so you can start to see.

Be free of self destructive thoughts and emotional triggering. You die the moment you stop learning, regardless of if your physical body is alive or not. Be an eagle, see what others can't.

What an experiment we have been. Created and destroyed many times. Movies gave us a lot of clues about our maker. Also our maker is created by the real AL (EL). The Chemist (The ultimate ALCHEMIST). The one and only, The ALCHEMIST that is within us all. The above artwork is about those that have kept us from recognizing the alchemist within.

> Go in front of the mirror and take a look at the alchemist. Meditate regularly so you can feel the alchemist. Until it becomes a habit of feeling it while conscious. That way you can practice the art of alchemy in every step of the way.

*I deliberately left this seemingly scary artwork for last. As a last reminder that to obtain **the key**, you must first go through the thorns (dark agents of your soul and within your mind). There is no other way but to face the ugly monsters within yourself. We all have those monsters inside. Some of us have defeated the inner monsters/shadows/wounds. You can too.*

WHO ARE YOU?

Did you find out yet?

Can you answer who you are without using words or thoughts? When you answer without words or thoughts, it will be the moment that you will be reborn (metaphorically).

*If you found this book useful in any way, a review on **Amazon** will be greatly appreciated.*

THANK YOU

FOOTNOTES

1. Government from Latin - *govern* = to govern to control, and *ment* = mind. Mind control or mind transplant. Since you are getting controlled, it means your mind is not your own.

2. A witch is a person who practices witchcraft. A witch is someone who actively practices magic rituals and spells. It is someone who has a spiritual connection such as a psychic medium or a tarot card reader. There is black or white magic. So, a witch can be a good or a bad person depending on if they use the magic for benevolent or malevolent purposes.

3. A binary code represents text, computer processor instructions, or any other data using a two-symbol system. "0"'s and "1's are the two-symbol system for the binary number system. The binary code assigns a pattern of binary digits, also known as bits, to each character, instruction, etc.

4. I used the word *sunrise* instead of *morning* as the word morning derives from "mourning". English language is very cunning. If you say 'morning' you start the day by dying instead of living. Little by little it adds onto your subconscious.

5. The Hypothalamic Pituitary Adrenal (HPA) axis is our central stress response system. The HPA axis is an eloquent and every-dynamic intertwining of the central nervous system and endocrine system. This system works in a fairly straight-forward manner. The HPA axis is responsible for the neuroendocrine adaptation component of the stress response.

6. Rise in Love is the correct way to say it. You only fall in hate.

7. I do not believe that apes are our ancestors 100%. Our species is a genetic manipulation of the DNA of a group of different extraterrestrial species including DNA from the primate mammals, which then homo sapiens was created, which is us.

8. Gaia is life. She is all, the very soul of the Earth. She is Goddess, by all accounts, inhabits the planet, offering life and nourishment to all her children. Her children are humans, animals, birds, insects, plants, oceans-rivers etc. Gaia is Earth.

9. Divine creator of all things. Religion calls it God, Science calls it physics,

Spirituality calls it energy(consciousness). But it's the same thing.

10. Hippocrates was a Greek physician who lived from 460 B.C to 375 B.C. At a time when most people attributed sickness to superstition and the wrath of gods, Hippocrates taught that all forms of illness had a natural cause. He established the 1st intellectual school devoted to teaching the practice of medicine. For this, he is widely known as the "father of medicine"

11. Max Karl Ludwig Planck, was a German theoretical physicist, the most influential of modern physics, as he discovered quantum energy, which won him the Nobel Prize in Physics in 1918.

12. Thoth or Hermes, was a god of the moon, of reckoning, of learning, and of writing. He was held to be the inventor of writing, the creator of languages, the scribe, interpreter, and adviser of the gods, and representative of the sun god Re/Ra/Rah.

13. Being hurt mentally or emotionally it's all on you. Another person cannot hurt your feelings without your cooperation. Your feelings are yours, how can someone else hurt them? You are hurt the moment you beLIEve yourself to be.

14. Mer = Light, Ka = Spirit, Ba = Body . MERKABA is an energetic field surrounding the body. Used during meditation, it is a source of Power and Enlightenment. Used to transcend to other dimensions and realities. MERKABA is a vehicle of spiritual ascension.

RESOURCES

The Biology of Belief by Bruce H. Lipton..........................

Physical fitness by Arnold Ehret....................................

You Are The One by Pine G. Land

Rebuild Yourself From Within by J.J. and TAMO

YOU ARE THE REMEDY by Anna Replica

The convoluted Universe by Dolores Cannon....................

Between death and life by Dolores Cannon.....................

The science of self-empowerment by Gregg Braden...........

Perception Deception by David Icke..............................

I AM the open door by Ascended Masters........................

YOU ARE THE ONE by Pine G. Land

The ancient secret of the flower of life by Drunvalo
Melchizedek..

Blue Blood True Blood by Stewart A. Swerdlow................

Earth-Pleiadeans key to the living library by Barbara
Marciniak...

Bringers of the Dawn by Barbara Marciniak.....................

Phantom Time Theory from www.misteriousuniverse.com....

Adventures in the afterlife by William Buhlman ......

www.theserpentsway.com

AFTERWORD

What a journey it has been. Assuming you learned something new or your way of thinking/believing got challenged. I have given the book to a few people and some of them don't believe certain things, some wanted to read what they only understand and some others wanted more.

This book is written for those that want to learn more and for those that may know and innerstand the contents of this book but need a refresher.

We all need a refresher of information or else we fall in the comfortable zone. I even learned to see certain things from a different perspective while in the process of writing it. This book and any book out there are not written for those refusing to let new information challenge their beLIEfs. What's the point of reading books?

To learn new information of course. Deep down, everyone is willing to learn more, we all have it in our DNA to want to expand our consciousness.

THE UNIVERSE IS ALL YOURS.

ABOUT THE AUTHOR

Saimir X. Kercanaj

Saimir is a passionate writer and an artist. After many years working for corporations, he decided to pursue what makes him happy, which is art/creating. He is on a mission to spread knowledge and innerstanding about life.

Saimir feels he must share his gifts with the world because he truly believes that we are all one and deserve to be happy and united. Working for many corporations, having dealt with thousands of people during his lifetime and with his inner knowing, gave him tremendous insight about the world and everything in it.

He will continue spreading truth in hopes that all humanity unites and becomes ONE.

Other books by the author

Made in the USA
Columbia, SC
03 November 2024

45598387R00130